TEENAGER'S GUIDE TO BECOMING A MILLIONAIRE

By J.R.

THE FUTURE BELONGS TO ME!

ACKNOWLEDGMENTS AND CREDITS

To all the teenagers and sophisticated adults who contributed to the many, many revisions of this book may each of you reward yourself for helping to make this book possible.

Special thanks goes to my neighbor, Pamela Parsons, a writer and editor, in North Barrington, Illinois, who spent so many hours with constructive criticism on layout and structure. I would recommend her to anyone wanting advice on how to structure a book. aromaticthymes@mac.com

Special thanks to Susan Kramer from Eagle Press, Crystal Lake, Illinois for the Typography of our printed book, Graphic Design and concept of our cover to help capture a teenager's imagination. Info@EaglePressCL.net.

Special thanks to Beatrice Sanquino at Beasanguino@gmail.com for her skill as a licensed Spanish translator and interpreter. You can judge the quality of her work by reading it against the English version, and the future French and German versions.

Special thanks to Julie Salisbury for her knowledge of knowing which publisher would most likely be interested in your subject matter. If you are a first time author consider contacting her at contact@inspiresbook.com

Special thanks to Trace Krug for his contribution to artwork on the cover Trace_k@sbcglobal.net along with Justin Sachs at www.JSachs.com

First published in the United States in 2006 by Eagle Press in partnership with author, John Ratkovich, 171 S. Main Street, Crystal Lake, IL 60014.
Self published John Ratkovich 2012 USA

Copyright © 2006-2014 John Ratkovich

All rights reserved. No part of this book may be reproduced or used in any form or by any means graphic, electronic or mechanical including photocopying, recording, taping or information storage and retrieval system without written permission of John Ratkovich, author.

The information contained in this book is given without warranty and, while every precaution has been taken in compiling the book, neither the author nor publisher assume any responsibility or liability whatsoever to any person or entity with respect to any errors which may exist in the book, nor for any loss of monies which may occur as the result of information or performance of any stocks or ideas described in the book.

Library of Congress Catalog No. TX 6-402-340
ISBN #10 06 155 341 139 and ISBN #13 978 06 155 341 38
Teenagers Guide to Becoming a Millionaire.

TABLE OF CONTENTS

"INTRODUCTION"

Hello Message From J. R 1
This Book Was Written For You! 3
Why did I Write This Book? 5
Keeping Your Interest 9

Chapter 1
"Fly Like An Eagle"

You Can Do It! 11
Give Yourself Permission To Be Rich 11
The Point Of It All 15

Chapter 2
"The Meat Of The Book"

Rules Of Engagement 17
Why The Two Rules Work 19
Complex Patents 24
Beliefs -vs- Ideas 27
Parents 30
Starting Today 31
How Fortunate You Are 34
Show Me The Money 36
Just Like The Old Western Movies 38

Chapter 3
"The Practical Stuff"

Your First Full Time Job 41
Clothes 42
How Not To Get Hired 45
Paying For Your Costume 48

Chapter 4
"Your Personal Choices"

Taking Orders or Giving Orders 51
Being Your Own Person 54
Forgive Yourself 56
Money Reserves 60
Have Someone Else Pay Your
   College Tuition 60
In Your Own Neighborhood .63

Chapter 5
Helpful Hints As You Mature

Business Hints: 75
   Examples 76
   Handwriting Analysis 77
Personal Hints:
   Boy-Girl Relationships 78
   Problem Solving Between the Sexes 80
   Several Rules for the Men .82
   Several Rules for the Women 83
   Two Forks and a Dessert 84
   Dealing with a Bully 84
   Police Record 86
   Sexting, Texting & Criminal Acts 88

Chapter 6
References-Selection-Sources

Selected Readings 95
Resale Shops for Suits and Dresses 95
Sources for Tailor Made Clothing 96
Selected Speculative Stocks 96
Basic Lesson on How to Choose a Stock to Buy 98
Sources for Gold or Silver Coins / ETFs 99
Caddie Scholarships to College 100
Macrobiotics 100
Emerging Billion Dollar Industries 100
   Two Examples 101

Chapter 7
"Beyond Our Borders"

Teenager's In Other Countries 103

Chapter 8
Summary

The Future 107

Chapter 9
"Millionaires Guide To Becoming A Teenager"

My Next Book 109
University of Millionaires 109

Chapter 10
"Personal Growth Pages"

Individual Goals 111
My Improvements 112
Investments 112
Congratulations 114

Prelude

This is a summary to the next three Appendixes 115

Appendix I

Brief Explanation of Metaphysics 117

Appendix II

Healing Yourself 121
Breakthroughs 127
Balancing the Universe 138
Metaphysics Upsets a Lot of Readers 142

Appendix III

A Good-bye Message from J.R. 151

Preface

"Many 35 year old adults,
currently living from paycheck to
paycheck, look back at high school and regret
not having an experienced adult give them
guidance on how to become wealthy."

*The core idea that gains wealth is that you
reward yourself because
you feel good about yourself.*

*"In America, Every Bird Is Free,
To Land On Any Tree"*

- anonymous

Introduction

"A Hello Message From J.R."

Hello students, this is where we begin our journey. Picture yourself in your own room at the end of the day. For the next hour let's settle in for an emotional, imaginary, entertaining and educational ride into your future. My suggestion is that you speed-read the entire English or Spanish section in one sitting. Take a yellow or red marking pen and touch the paragraphs that take your interest as you glance through the Chapters.

Once you are at the end then you can choose what to go back to and gradually you will see this book is designed for continual use on an on going basis. It is not for just a "once through" and put on the shelf. I am going to give you over 75 years of what I have learned as a father of 3 sons and 3 daughters and ten grandchildren. There should be something just for you in the book that could bring more "certainty" into your teenage years and evaporate some of the anxieties that each of you might have.

Now picture yourself as a grown man or woman and ask yourself the following question, "Each morning at sunrise, do I want to be looking out at the ocean from my 10th story condo balcony in Hawaii (or Florida) or preparing for my commute to the local factory in Chicago or Los Angeles where I will be punching an hourly time card"?

A limited number of people are born into this world with talent in music, theater, or sports. They earn a great deal of money performing for others. Then there are the rest of us! We have average parents, a normal upbringing and eventually graduate from high school or college. Now we have to go find a full time job.

The idea of having a rewarding "enjoy-going-to-work-each-day" career, rather than working just to make enough money to get by is the ultimate goal for all of us. However, until you are convinced about a specific career, or your special niche, why not simply target a career of making as much money as possible in the shortest period of time? With this flexible thinking, by the time you are 35 years old, you could have more money in the bank than you can spend. If this idea turns on your juices, then let's relax and go through each section in this book, one paragraph at a time.

THIS BOOK WAS WRITTEN FOR YOU!

Many "How To Be A Millionaire" books have been written with guidance for adult investors, but few exist for teenagers. This book was written for you - a high school kid who probably hasn't given a thought about what you are going to do a few years from now when you have to feed yourself.

I have observed, to a large extent, that you guys and gals focus on spending most of your money on items like concert tickets, and fashionable teen clothes. The idea of reducing your spending - so that by the time you are 35 years old, your bank account holds more lawfully earned money than you or your relatives could ever imagine - is probably too "out there" for most of you. However, maybe you are "special." Maybe you are unique and stand out from the crowd. Maybe you are a teenager, who has sufficient common sense to take my suggestions seriously.

Pause for a moment. Notice, if you recently have started to think about the future, especially if you have had the joyous and exciting experience of meeting the first love of your life at school or in the neighborhood. It could also be that some other new viewpoint has suddenly taken you out of childhood to semi maturity. Consider allowing yourself to absorb the significance of the ideas in this book as foundation stones to build a secure financial future for your potential family or profession.

Look at Mom and Dad. They may be very successful and can, in a seemingly effortless manner, provide you with a peaceful home environment and also meet all of your financial needs. However, some of you may have parents who do not speak fluent English. Some of you may have parents that do not have an adequate education to get a decent paying job, or who might live in fear of losing their job due to lay off. Maybe you are a victim of a home environment that has its share of problems such as a single parent situation, daily arguments every time you come home, or even more serious problems. Maybe you feel "all alone." Most of you are in between these extremes. Some of the suggestions in this book may give you a new direction so you can then assume more control over your life.

WHY DID I WRITE THIS BOOK?

My initial assumption was that you teenagers could care less about my motivation in writing this book.

Then, while all the editing and proofreading was in process, the professionals assisting me kept encouraging me to tell my "tale" without getting all "weepy eyed" during the story.

I was still thinking that "the event" which occurred to get the whole process going would be too boring to any teenager. Then I was told that everyone likes to hear the story behind the scenes. I asked around, and sure enough, curiosity is a powerful motivational force.

The light bulb suddenly went on.

I saw where you teenagers should be aware of how single experiences in your future (as early as tomorrow) could precipitate a hidden talent that you were born with. Currently, you might enjoy drawing cartoons, futuristic airplanes, women's clothes or jewelry. You might enjoy telling ridiculous riddles or shaggy dog stories to cause a lot of laughter. You may be the class clown, or you may have the ultimate in hand and eye coordination on a skateboard.

When you demonstrate whatever superior natural talent you have on an everyday basis, you probably are not even aware of the potential of that gift. You probably have never viewed your special skill as being anything unusual or as a foundation to make a fortune in money and personal satisfaction. One day in the future, while fooling around with your friends, someone says "Hey, John or Mary, you really have a talent. Why don't you create something with it?

This is what happened to me at age 70. Hopefully, it will happen to you slightly earlier.

A High School teacher at Taft High School on the N.W. side of Chicago called me up one day and asked if I would speak at Career Day.

On the Career day I was to speak, I was dressed in my three-piece suit, white shirt and red tie, which is my standard dress each day at the office.

Now the plot thickens: I had no idea what to talk about. The request for my appearance had only come to me one day earlier. Apparently the assigned speaker had an emergency and I was the substitute. I thought I would start out by asking the students what was the current "buzz" on campus and "wing it" from there.

The 17-18 year olds filed into the classroom and after seating the teacher introduced another speaker and me.

I was designated as first to speak. Just as I was about to say something, in walks a Jock who is built like a star athlete. The teacher asked him if he was late because he was visiting with some speaker from a previous class.

He casually sauntered to the seat furthest from the speaker's table and put one leg up on the desk. His description of the previous classroom speakers was "they suck". He went on to question why the school wastes the student time by insisting that the students listen to boring strangers talk, talk and talk about what they do each day at work. Everything he said made clear sense to me.

I started by asking questions about the current "buzz" around school, and I was told a few things that everyone was talking about. At an appropriate moment, I used what the student had said to bring up my objective of finding out... who wants to make lots and lots of money? I then spoke about how being wealthy is not something to be embarrassed about. I spoke about the two rules of "giving more than you get so you will get more than you give" and "you can't help someone else without helping yourself". There was some modest exchange of views between the students. The session ended and the teacher asked if anyone had any questions. No one spoke up.

The teacher thanked me for speaking and it was obvious it was over. Then the Jock at the rear of the room stood up and started clapping very, very slowly with a least one-second pause between each clap. He was looking me right in the eye. He stopped clapping and without a word he again slandered by me with full eye contact and flicked his chin down like surviving warriors do in the movies after a battle to give recognition of having "bonded" or connected to their fellow survivors. He then disappeared into the crowd in the hallway.

He had pushed my hot button. I could not recall ever having been so emotionally overwhelmed and temporarily unfocused in all my 70 plus years.

It was that evening that I started laying out this book because one or more of the ideas I presented had touched this young man. If this young man saw the sense in what I had said then there was a message that I had to get out to the all young people.

End of story. Hope you felt what I was trying to convey to you. You too will have an experience like this in your lifetime. When it happens remember this message of mine and run with it. "Be all you can be" with the talent you were born with. Don't hold back. That will be "your" moment.

KEEPING YOUR INTEREST

I have limited the scope of what you are about to read because I thought it best to have something brief and encouraging rather than a text book which tries to be all things to all teenagers in one huge "know it all" book.

I will only just touch on how to invest, as that has been well covered in other books that you can research in the library or on the Internet. Most of you should be able to finish this book in one reading. If you want to write me with suggestions on how to improve or elaborate on the subjects I presented send your correspondence to me at:

American Home Finance, Inc.

830 W. Northwest Highway
Palatine, Illinois 60067.

If you mail it in, I will then send you a free copy of the next revised edition of this book – if one is ever written - as compensation. If you would rather have a dialogue with me, just go to:

**TheFutureBelongsToMe.com
Jr@TheFutureBelongsToMe.com**

and I will do my best to answer your questions the same as I have done, and still do, with my own kids.

Chapter 1
"FLY LIKE AN EAGLE"

"Anyone who has struggled with poverty knows how expensive it is to be poor."
-Anonymous

You Can Do It!

This chapter deals with your starting to think about having the choice to stand still or go forward.

Imagine what your relatives would say to you if you announced, "I am going to make a career out of becoming a millionaire!" Since some of them are living from paycheck to paycheck, they may simply ignore you. Others will chuckle to themselves, or roll their eyes. Some may make fun of you out of envy or some other insecurity. Just the thought of you making more money in one year than they have made in 20 years may cause one of them to say things to you that will hurt.

Most of you have relatives who love and respect you, and they admire your high aspirations. However, if any relative or adult cautions you about succeeding beyond just getting a job and working for someone else for the next 40 years, ask yourself, " Just what have they accomplished with their life?" How qualified are they to discourage me from developing my full potential? Are they driving a rusted out Honda or a bright shiny Mercedes?"

Give Yourself Permission To Be Rich

I am going to assume from the start that you realize that you have just as much freedom of choice in America to be a millionaire as you do to be an Olympic swimmer, a Golden Globe nominee, a Justice of the Supreme Court or another legitimate profession. Let's get rid of any negative preconceived notion that there is something wrong with being wealthy.

America is called the land of opportunity. You have probably read in the newspapers about the illegal immigrants who risk their lives to gain entry into the USA. They want to stay here because our system encourages everyone to pursue their financial dreams under the protection of our laws. Consider allowing yourself the freedom of self-expression to examine and anticipate the potential of every new idea that comes into your thought. Rumor has it that famous actor Harrison Ford was a carpenter working on the original set of the Star Wars I movie lot before he auditioned for the part of the wise guy pilot in that Oscar winning movie.

When you see an opportunity, do something about it! Don't let it pass and leave you empty-handed. It is the same as when you challenge yourself to create a new web site or try to sell something in your neighborhood just to see how far you can go. When in doubt, consider taking a chance so that you don't look back and always wonder what would have happened if you had only put out a little bit more of effort to see if the idea in your head could actually work.

This is a real challenge for most teenagers since your close friends will probably discourage you from exploring your new idea since they don't appreciate or understand the foresight you have. So what do you do? You find a quiet place and start getting the idea down on paper. After a short period of time you will get a positive or negative feeling and surge forward or back off. Either way - at least you tried.

For example:

Should you travel to Alaska to work in a fishing cannery for the summer or just continue working around the bike shop in your hometown until something better comes along?

Here is a simple exercise to help you when such opportunities arise:

Just like I suggested at the beginning of the introduction, close your eyes, just for a moment, and see what thoughts immediately come to your mind. If it is the opposite sex then go with that. Vision is the key to opening the door to some significant money making idea. For example, what product are girls talking about today? Maybe you can improve it or design a new one. If your vision is about sports or some other achievement, try to let your mind run in an uninhibited manner to see if it takes you down an unexplored river of IDEAS. Maybe you will see yourself designing a new lipstick or perfume or heat activated paper that you can write on with a touch of your finger rather than a pen or pencil. Your job is to discover what good IDEA is right in front of you. Once you feel a high comfort level, move on it.

You will find the above exercise to be especially helpful in your senior year when decisions about your future are so important. Your mental job is to DISCOVER what is best for you, not to CREATE IT. Creating the best idea belongs to the Boss. Remember, every tribe on this planet calls the Boss by a different name, but He or She or It already knows what would be the best thing for you to pursue just at that moment. This exercise is a good way to tune into what has been created especially for you!

Let's get back to the goal of you giving you permission to make a career out of making money, just to make money. Being a millionaire is nothing special. All it means is that you have more money to spend than most of the other people around you. By itself, it does not make you any better than the other guy. Your sports heroes, your concert idols, your family physician and other wealthy men and women are just ordinary people the same as you. They all probably went through high school experiencing the same highs and lows you have. They simply chose - or fell into - a career that was uniquely suited to their physical or intellectual abilities, and from that, they made a lot of money.

You are entitled to do the same in whatever field you choose, but if you don't have a specific profession in mind at this moment, then you might as well just make money - more money than you can spend - by following the suggestions in this book until a more exciting career choice comes into clearer focus.

Allow yourself to mentally develop a pattern for making money the same way as you would train yourself to physically memorize a pattern in karate. The ideas in this book will give you a blueprint to work with to help you get started. Later on, you will modify what I have suggested to meet your individual needs. If you don't grasp or feel the significance of what I am suggesting, then back off since you are not yet in the zone for this type of discipline. It will come in time. When you feel something is right for you, then you will know what I am talking about.

The Point Of It All

For those of you who take this book seriously, my objective is to make you a millionaire, not necessarily because you have a special talent that an audience will pay to see you demonstrate, but because you have developed your ability to see with your eyes and hear with your ears. Seeing with your eyes and hearing with your ears means you work with the talent you have. You play to your strengths and stop putting yourself down because you are not an athletic super jock or the perfect size 4. The other guy or gal might invent a fantastic new computer, while you invent a new T-shirt slogan or design a new dress or a new improved squeeze cap for toothpaste wherein you don't have to remove the cap before spreading the toothpaste onto the brush. All three are equally useful, interesting or desirable in their own way. You can walk tall with you head held high because your creativity is just as good as the other guy. Your opinion of yourself is the only opinion that is important. If you don't accept this concept you will never allow yourself to develop to your full potential.

All of you, in the range of normal unimpaired intelligence, can discipline yourselves to focus on the goal of being a millionaire. You can still fulfill a "calling" such as the Peace Corps, which does not pay much. You could still become a millionaire in your spare time by bringing new business ideas to that 3rd world country while you are there. The difference is that it may take you longer. After all, there are only so many hours in the day you can work for someone else and then try to develop your own business. Most of you are too young to give yourself permission to be a millionaire and your family members are not thinking about the subject, so someone else has to motivate you. This book is your permission to make a career out of becoming a millionaire. If you learn these lessons well, someday in the future you will give your sons and daughters the same permission to develop their full potential in whatever career they choose.

Chapter 2
"THE MEAT OF THE BOOK"

"Whether rich or poor, it is better to have money."

Rules Of Engagement

There are two rules I want you to memorize for becoming a millionaire:

- The first rule is *"The more you give, the more you get"*.
- The second rule is *"You can't help someone else without helping yourself"*.

Every adult millionaire reading this book, who made his or her money legally, knows what I am talking about.

I suspect some of you are snickering at the concept of giving rather than getting, but the net result of the above two rules is that you feel good about yourself. Feeling good about yourself is a winning formula in all walks of our human experience. When you feel good about yourself, your self-esteem and confidence rises. At the same time your intuition and skill level seem to increase because you see things more clearly. You find that you are suddenly able to make just the right financial decisions, such as buying a stock or a piece of real estate at just the right time.

If you are in sports, that will be the day you will pitch the no hitter, execute the perfect block to free your halfback for a long run, score a 5.9 on the parallel bars or run the 200-meter in 21.74 seconds. For the girls, you may design the perfect new dress for that special occasion or perform as you never have before, whether it be as an equestrian, actress, musician or academic. It is like an emotional "release." When you just go with the flow instead of being fearful or hesitant, magic happens.

When you "Give more than you get" the following reactions generally occurs. Out of 10 people that you do something nice for (something out of the ordinary where you did not have any obligation to be so generous with your time or money) one of them will see your efforts as a sign of weakness to be exploited. That person will probably do a number on you, which will cost you emotionally and maybe financially. (The upside is now you know to never trust that person again.) In this scenario of letting your guard down and being taken advantage of, you have to just accept the hit and walk away. However, eight out of the ten will say things that are pleasant and it will be a modest emotional achievement. The last one of the ten will be super appreciative and say things to you that gold and diamonds cannot buy. You will feel so good about yourself you may get "weepy eyed" as you feel a warm sense of internal satisfaction for having done something unselfish.

Because you feel so good about yourself you will be on a kind of a high and are likely to make just the right move - financial or otherwise.

Most of your teachers, in or out of high school, experience all three of these reactions from their students on a regular basis. They know the joy of seeing one or two of you reach your full academic potential, and in that sense they are educational millionaires, guiding you to make the world a better place to live in. The only reason they are not putting their energy towards accumulating diamonds and dollars outside of their teaching career is that they have chosen not to do so. Some few may be independently wealthy from an inheritance or an invention or an apartment building investment, but most teachers see their students' intellectual success to be more important than their own financial success. Of those teachers you admire, consider looking that teacher in the eye the next time you are in private, or in a group, with him or her, and sincerely say "Thank you!"

Why The Two Rules Work

II have to qualify the things said in the last paragraph. Nice things do not always come your way just because you were unselfish and helped someone else. What happens is you feel so good about yourself that your uncertain personal BELIEFS or hang-ups (fear, anger, self condemnation, revenge, etc.) temporarily evaporate from your thought. The result is you suddenly see new, sparkling good IDEAS right in front of you, like a field of spring flowers and you're entitled to pick as many as meet your needs.

Here is an example of how my son in law, who has a reasonable understanding of the distinction between IDEAS and BELIEFS, solved something bothering his children and he will probably make a lot of money off the patent he has filed.

He has two young girls who like to color with colored marking pens. He was concerned with the girls' frustration over the cap getting lost under the furniture, the pens drying out, the 3 year old not having the strength to pull the cap off the pen, and his own anxiety over the 3 year old choking on the loose cap. His was an unselfish concern for others. He was trying to help someone else, and, according to Rule #2, - "You can't help someone else without helping yourself." his mind cleared itself of BELIEFS (anger, frustration, irritation etc.) and he was able to see the answer to his problem. The answer had been there all along, but he just could not see it through the fog of BELIEFS.

His solution - Instead of putting the cap on the marker, he put the marker on the cap! He took the box the markers came in and fastened the caps upside down in the bottom of the box. The young children can now force the marker into the cap since they have a large surface to grip with their tiny hands. The children are happy to have markers that are not dried out and Dad is talking to the manufacturers of colored marking pens about a joint venture.

Because he tried to help someone else, his mind was cleared, just like a rainstorm clears the air of dust so you can see the stars at night. Consider taking a chance. Try this concept with some set of circumstances that you think needs to be changed for the better. Within that effort, you are automatically trying to help someone else - even if it appears that you are just trying to help yourself. As you let your thoughts roam into new territory, IDEAS start to appear on your internal visual screen and you automatically go to an emotional high and the solution to your problem becomes obvious.

For example: Who knows, you may figure out how to take a paper napkin, put a slightly tacky plastic Saran like plastic film on the back of it (to protect your shirt while drinking coffee or soda), and sell it to McDonalds as a throw away bib for eating messy hamburgers and drinks while driving in the car. Or you might figure out a way to just spray a light glue like you find on Post-It note pads onto one side of a roll of toweling with the logo of the advertiser on the other side. Imagine getting rid of the waste of thousands of napkins that people take and throw out without ever using. Here you would have a bib that clings to your vest or shirt, protects your clothes, and then peels off with the slightest effort without leaving any residue on your clothes. You may see this as just another selfish idea, but it is really helping a whole industry including the "tree huggers" trying to save the forests.

How about figuring out how to get rid of the problem of the chocolate stains on your clothes and the mess on your hands while eating a chocolate ice cream bar? Consider making the plastic wrapper unfold like a banana peel with the inside lower one half of the plastic wrapper having a napkin or tissue to absorb the melting chocolate. Simple idea, but very complicated to engineer.

What if you earned the eternal gratitude of exhausted and bored husbands who have to attend street Art Fairs all summer long with their spouse? They have to stand idle in front of the vendor's booth for 20 minutes while their significant-other studies every piece of jewelry or coffee mug. Why not design a flop or pull down seat that attaches to the light or telephone pole in front of the booths? This could also allow pregnant women to attend Art Fairs or other exhibits knowing they could sit down occasionally.

If your Shop Teacher at High School could help you with the design you could price the design out with a local company who does Metal Stampings. You could then make an appointment with the City Planning Department Manager for the City you live in and present the idea to be used in all Tourist areas or sites like a Summer Food Fair. The sales point would be that the Mayor of your city would get publicity and may get more votes towards re-election because he or she was trying to do something for the Public. You in turn would earn a significant amount of money as Broker or sales company with the actual manufacturing being done by people already in the business. Everyone would win!

If you have an idea that you think has sufficient Novelty to warrant a Patent consider contacting me at JR@TheFutureBelongsToMe.com. I will give you my best advice at that time.

My last leaf will probably fall off my tree in another 10-12 years so I am not looking to steal anyone's patentable ideas and get involved with aggravation and law suits.

Who knows, maybe we can start a Teenagers' Blog to discuss new ideas for Patents. The proof of you originating the idea in the first place would be in the date on the Blog and this would retard anyone else from blatantly stealing your idea. You would have to back it up with drawings or some prototype to show when you first started working on the project.

We could limit it to just teenagers and develop the idea in a competition with some kind of an award once a year for the best idea.

Even if nothing comes from the above remember what you just read here. This flamboyant approach to using your eyes to see with and your ears to hear with is what will give you reason to get out of bed each morning with a "snap". It makes for an exciting reason to get to school or to try out something new. It sure beats dragging yourself to the bathroom to start another dull meaningless day.

I am probably repeating myself, but consider allowing

yourself to look at all the physical objects around you and see if you can see some room for improvement. An example of what I am talking about would be the coffee you drink at Starbucks. A few years ago a person your age had a hard time holding the hot coffee cup and trying to wrap napkins around the cup to protect his hand from the heat. He went home and invented the "slip on" thin cardboard sleeve that is currently in use. He probably sold the idea to Starbucks and he is probably paid a penny for each one they purchase or use. He probably earns several million dollars a year in Royalties.

Why don't you invent a way to put a plastic propeller on the inside of a glass jar of peanut butter? The propeller would be attached to the underside of the cap and every time you unscrewed or screwed the cap on it would mix the peanut butter. This would avoid the tough job of using a knife to stir the peanut butter before using.

If you really wanted to get creative why not make the peanut butter jar out of soft plastic so you could massage or squeeze the bottle to mix the oil into the peanuts. Once mixed, you could take the small cap off and spread just what quantity you want on the bread. Success with either of these ideas would make you the "big man or woman on campus" for a short period of time.

Keep in mind that to secure a patent you need your new idea to have special Novelty for the Patent Office to approve it for you alone. Think for a moment on the concepts of the propeller or the squeeze bottle. Which one or both strikes you as having a Novelty that is different from anything you can see on the shelf of the grocery store today?

Complex Patents

Here is a Patent idea for those studying Engineering. How many times have you lost your grip on a bar of soap in the shower and after dropping the bar you had to deal with the broken chips and the delay in getting out of the shower?

As an experiment, take a bar of soap and cut or break it up into 4-5 sections about 1 to 2 inches in height. Get a coffee cup saucer from the kitchen and put the chunks on the saucer with just enough water to cover the entire saucer. The next day toss the water and observe the smooth surface on the bottom of the soap and the jagged edges on the top.

The jagged edges are for you to have a stronger grip on the soap bar and the smooth side is for use against the skin. You can probably get a Copyright for 3 years with the Patent Office, but that is not going to make your fortune.

As an Engineer you have to figure out how to build the machinery or the tools that will adapt to present day machinery. This is a Patentable idea you can then sell to a soap manufacture or maybe you and Dad can start up a shop and Dad will suddenly have a retirement program that no one is going to take away from him. This will be your way of paying Dad back for all the love and caring he has given you in the past.

If you go to any strangers for help with this idea then have a written statement on a piece of paper for them to sign that merely says you spoke with them on that particular day about the idea of "designing a machine or tools to manufacture a bar of soap with a smooth side for the skin and a jagged side for better grip pressure with the hand" this will insure you by 90% that the idea will not be stolen from you by the 3rd party. I would like to be your first customer when you make your first production run. Consider calling it "Rocky Mountain Bar Soap".

The following is an example of what I am talking about, taken from www.About.com.

In 1994 Kathryn Gregory, now a teenager from Bedford, Massachusetts, became an inventor and an entrepreneur at the age of ten. According to "Wristies", "On a cold and snowy winter's day, 10 year old Kathryn Gregory was out building a snow fort when her wrists started to hurt because they were cold and wet. She remedied the problem by inventing "Wristies", and wore them under her coat and mittens."

Kathryn invented and trademarked "Wristies". "Wristies" are protective winter gear that is designed to be worn under your coat and gloves to block the snow, wind, and cold from entering any unprotected gaps.

Also while a kid inventor, Kathryn Gregory started "Wristies", Inc., a company to manufacture and sell "Wristies". The young entrepreneur has made deals with the Girl Scouts, Federal Express, and McDonald's. In 1997, Kathryn Gregory became the youngest person to sell on QVC, the television shopping show.

You too can feel "the pain" of some inconvenient or threatening situation and think about designing something to lessen the discomfort. This could be a moment of "discovery" on your part and lead to a generous lifestyle instead of a living from paycheck to paycheck. Even if you are only a waitress maybe you could suggest to your boss that he have 8" x 11" belt towels for the waitresses and bus boys to wear that not only are useful to quickly wipe up spills, but have embroidery on them that state "WE HOPE YOU COME BACK!" Phil G. THE OWNER.

Go home and get a finger towel from Mom and find an embroidery company out of the Yellow Pages. They will charge you $8 - 10.00 for the embroidery. Show it to your boss. He may go for the idea. If not he will suddenly see you as a person rather than a number and possibly promote you to supervisor.

The athletes, mathematicians, violinists, and writers reading this will recognize this as "being in the zone." It happens when your mind is temporarily immune to the human aggravation around you. Your focus is so directed that the answer to the best move on the chessboard of life seems clear and visually correct even before you make it.

If you allow yourself to appreciate this distinction between IDEAS and BELIEFS you will grow into adulthood earning money by discovering IDEAS and being a leader in your field. If you are open to exploring some new exciting IDEAS and refuse to be limited by others' negative BELIEFS, (i.e. "It will never fly.") then logically you will use them to reward yourself in the months to follow to get out of problems or make more money.

On the down side, these insights usually start to fade quickly. Your mind then allows your old BELIEFS to seep back in and you then drift back to your old routine self. However, you have now irreversibly moved one or two squares forward on the millionaire trail of success. If you play Monopoly, it is the same as moving your piece one or two squares closer to "Boardwalk" or "Park Place."

When I mention IDEAS vs. BELIEFS, try to appreciate the fact that even most adults can't grasp the entire significance of the concept. This is pretty sophisticated stuff and most adults equate it to "trying to nail Jell-O to the wall". Most adults don't want to take the time to think it through because it might challenge their own fixed, rigid belief system. I thought about it for some time before even including it in this book. I decided that since your youthful mind is open to everything new, I should at least let you know the subject exists. Most of you teenagers will just surf over this entire concept and that is permissible. However, maybe, there are one or two of you who might want to learn a little extra about IDEAS and BELIEFS, so I have put a more in depth analysis in the Appendix I and II section of this book under "Brief Explanation of Metaphysics." If you are now wondering why I addressed this subject at all in a book on money making, it is because it can be the foundation of all your future success both personally and monetarily, same as it has been for me.

BELIEFS constantly change so don't rely on them. Good IDEAS never change so you can rely on them. Remember, "Only good IDEAS exist. Bad ideas are just BELIEFS in disguise."

BELIEFS
Constantly Changing:
Fear of the future

Some Results:
Bottom of the Food Chain
No Real Friends
Guilt, Shame, Anger
   Revenge
Short Term Marriage
Children Who Don't Want Anything to do with you

IDEAS
Never Change:
Wisdom and Understanding

Some Results:
Certainty
Joyful Days
Sincere Long Term Companionship
Respect from Your Family

Supportive Diagram

Beliefs vs. Ideas

Once you have tried to grasp the distinction between IDEAS and BELIEFS, you either become confused because it's just " too much" with your limited exposure to the Truth, or else you sense a certainty and calm quite different from the usual uncertainty and fear about the future that most people live with until they die.

Once you understand, what I have been trying to convey, you step out of the cave of ignorance and into the sunlight of Truth. It is similar to the concept of a flower being unable to return to the seed it came from. You can only go forward and blossom to your full potential. Consider reading the above two paragraphs over a few times and think about IDEAS versus BELIEFS. It took me years to grasp what little I understand of the subject. However, if you can at least start to mentally toy with the concept, the end result will be a constant separation of problems into unchangeable good IDEAS, versus constantly changing BELIEFS. Understanding this difference alone will in all probability make you more money than you can spend. You will then undoubtedly have a most enjoyable adult experience with the people around you because they will observe your strength and serenity under pressure and compliment you for continually seeming to have a handle on things.

It is not important that you grasp the full significance of this book in one reading. However, starting today, consider pondering the concept that good IDEAS are permanent and never change but give you a feeling of peace and security. Good IDEAS (health, happiness, joy) are available to everyone and are unaffected by whatever aggravation you incur each day.

Human BELIEFS and rituals (fear, guilt, shame, anger) are constantly changing. They are man made concepts that hurt you as much as they sometimes help you because they keep you constantly off balance and agitated. This is a whole subject outside of this book, but if you at least know there is something to study to help you if you or your close friend's personal life is a mess, then I have done my job by merely mentioning it.

Let's talk about Rule #2; "You can't help someone else without helping yourself." We are talking about supportive effort on your part and not passing out physical items. To give someone the "shirt off your back," when it is the only shirt you have, is not a smart idea. To go out of your way to teach someone how to do something so they can earn a new shirt for their own back is a smart idea. Some of you already know how good you feel about yourself when you take the time to teach something to a younger brother or sister. They follow you around the house and look to you as the source of all knowledge. The day after you have taken the time to reach out to them is when you reward yourself by scoring the winning goal in that very, very important soccer game. It is the same feeling some older person got when they took the time to teach you when you were a child.

You don't go around giving poor people money since they will despise you for insulting them with your good intentions. You give them help through your time, patience and understanding to show them a way out of poverty. If they criticize you for not giving them money, they don't want to get out of poverty. They just want to spend your money on the same wasteful things they waste their money on now, be it gambling, alcohol, drugs, etc. Once again, if you extend yourself beyond your obligation, it may be no one will notice but yourself. However, because you feel good about yourself, you will find a way to reward yourself and move one notch closer to being a millionaire.

Put your thoughts down in a Journal or on the Note pages following this chapter.

Parents

For better or worse, all of us have or had one or more to deal with. For those of you whose parents were always "there when you needed them" and not just when it was "convenient" for them to help you, try to realize the significance of that charitable act on their part. If you are blessed with having eyes that see and ears that hear, you might consider telling them that you actually noticed their sacrifices.

You will make their day by letting them know that all their effort in tolerating your youthful, constantly changing viewpoint, was at least noticed by you. In keeping with the theme of this book, your parents will then feel so good about themselves they may reward themselves by making just the right decision in the market place of ideas. They might end up with a more secure financial future, ... all because of your having acknowledged what they did for you. Your sincere comments to your parents are "pay back time" and they may get weepy eyed with emotion that you recognize their sacrifices for your benefit.

Years from now when you have your own children consider "being there" when they need you and not just when it is "convenient" for you. The probability is that your children will grow to be more considerate and sincere, and may model themselves after you.

Sometimes however, when you are a parent, one of your teenagers may get off course. You as a parent will have to make an undesirable decision to not support a selfish, spoiled, foul mouth, 17-year-old, but you will figure that one out for yourself.

The bottom line of this type of posture with your future children is that you will feel so good about your efforts of "being there" when they need you, one way or another, you too will reward yourself in the market place of life. This cycle keeps repeating itself for generation after generation.

Consider asking advice from mom or dad or a successful relative about whether it is better to work for someone else the rest of your life or to go into business for yourself as soon as the opportunity presents itself. At your age, it is a bit scary to think about running your own business. The complex decisions about paying wages, rent, inventory, taxes, etc. are too much for you to clutter up your mind with. Just enjoy the ups and downs of being with your friends for now and know it will all work out if you start with saving your money today.

Starting Today

At your high school age, how do you get started when you haven't any money besides a few dollars from some part time work or a birthday gift from grandma? You do what every millionaire has done, who did not have a special talent at your age. You open a bank account. You then focus on accumulating money just as you would anything else, whether the collection is baseball cards, lipsticks, stamps or clippings on your favorite movie star. You do what ever it takes to find work of some kind so that at the end of each month you have more money in the bank this month than you had last month. It is like a game with yourself to see how much savings you can achieve without telling anyone your game plan. It is like seeing how many pushups you can do or how much weight you can press, or how many B+s or A's you can accumulate just to prove to yourself that you can do it. We see this in movies where the young hero drives himself or herself to perform some sport activity to prove he or she can do it. It is not for the admiration of a public audience, but for the self-respect of achievement or conquest when you are an audience of one (i.e. Karate Kid movie).

What about spending some money on your favorite activities? Each of you has to decide your priorities or what to spend on yourself and others for birthday gifts, etc. Even if you use up all your savings for a family emergency you can always start over. The emergency merely delays your arrival at your career objective of being a millionaire. On an everyday basis, consider the concept of letting your friends spend their money on cars, DVDs, jewelry and changing the color of their hair, while you save your money in the bank.

Consider not owning a car and use a bike for your transportation. At today's rates it will cost you at least $300 per month to finance a new car. Do everything you can to avoid owing anyone any money (except for a home mortgage a few years from now). If you want reliable transportation every time you need it, consider paying a friend

$20.00 for the gas when he or she drives on a double date. At today's costs your friend spends $16.00 every time he drives you 20 miles on a double date. That $16.00 includes gas, oil, repairs, insurance, & finance charges on the purchase price. By paying for more than the gas that is consumed on that date, your friend will go out of his or her way to drive you all over the place in the future since you are covering more than his or her immediate costs. A taxi would cost you $30. For the same 20-mile convenience, so you are constantly coming out ahead and you are avoiding the aggravation of owning a car with all the attached expenses, and you have a reputation around school for being generous.

What ever you do, don't underpay your friend for having given you a ride. You may reason that it is not costing your friend any more to take you along as a passenger so you don't have to pay him anything. That sort of childish reasoning will come back to bite you and you will lose your friend.

It costs around $.75 - $.80 per mile to operate a car in 2011 (currently changing almost daily.) The money your friend might have saved in his or her bank account has now disappeared while his or her car just wears or rusts out. Once anyone borrows money to buy a wasting asset like a car, there is never any extra money for savings. You can never get your career as a millionaire underway if you are constantly short of cash. If the car you buy, however, earns you money, for example - a taxi cab driver - you can justify the expense as an investment and also have wheels to get around on at the same time. Essentially, that approach brings you passengers to pay for your car plus leaves you with a few extra dollars to work with. Many taxi cab drivers started out with one car on borrowed money and ended up making so much money working 12 hours per day, seven days a week, that 5 years later they ended up with a fleet of 20 cabs and 20 employees. During the time the taxi cab driver was working 12 hours per day, he or she had access to the cab for personal use at very little extra expense. This was a win - win situation for the cab driver.

You need to decide while you read this book, which is more important. When you're 35 years old, is it going to be the earned privilege of being able to fly first class to Cancun, Mexico for the weekend, just because you feel like it? Or, is it going to be living in a rented apartment with a visit to the local movie theater or the pub being the highlight of your week? You can't have it both ways.

If you're weak, you will chose to spend instead of save and vote for the politician who promises you a larger unemployment check because getting fired or laid off goes hand in hand with not saving money in the bank. If you save, you have a sense of accomplishment and dominion over the things of this world. You are then your own person in a material sense. Keep in mind that being one's own person is much more expansive and rewarding than money in many cases, but that subject is outside the imaginary boundaries of this book.

How Fortunate You Are

Go look at yourself in the mirror right now. See the smile, the clear eyes, and the exuberance of your facial expression. Now, when the opportunity presents itself, look around at the faces of some of your classmates. Notice the quiet ones who just want to be left alone. Perhaps they have already "given up" because of some negative event that happened when they were younger. Until some teacher or mentor in or out of the classroom motivates them, they will probably just bobble along without any real joy in their life because the future doesn't hold any excitement for them. How about the students you know with the rings in their skin or have colored hair. Their need, might be to impress the world with how different they can look just because it is the current fashion and legitimate fun, or it might be so they can retaliate against mom and dad for constantly being on their back.

This is not meant to insult any ethnic group whose background demands the use of ornaments in the skin to identify their religious, family or geographic origins. That motive serves a legitimate purpose. However, if the goal of wearing ornaments in the skin is silent rebellion and that student is depressed about something in their personal lives, then all of what I have said is premature for them. Maybe you can help one of them out of their depression by saying something nice to one of them to make them feel they are not outcasts. Maybe one of them will actually smile instead of grinding their teeth and snarling at you. Maybe one of them will start to come back to center just because "you tried to help someone else." From such a minor charitable act on your part, such as saying something nice or reaching out with a friendly smile, you may feel so good that you will do something special for yourself to make a big financial difference in your future.

One example - testing my suggestion - would be at the next school dance, (if that sort of thing even exists anymore), consider asking the boy or girl whom no one will dance with for a dance. Look the person in the eye as you dance. They will be so excited at being accepted as worthy that they may even stumble on the dance floor. Observe how good you feel about yourself after the dance. Your internal satisfaction or joy that accompanies such a charitable act will give you a clue as to why I have enjoyed taking the time to write this book in the first place.

Show Me The Money

Let's say that most of you have $300 to $500 in the bank from gifts and earnings. The normal thing for a parent or guardian to do is to encourage you to be very conservative and just leave it alone in a savings account to earn a pittance of interest. This can be a good idea once you are older and have obligations to care for a family. It is not necessarily the best approach when you are a teenager who wants to make his or her mark early in his or her career of becoming a millionaire.

Some friends or family may tell you that $500 is not enough to invest in the stock market or some other investment. Each of us has to work with what we have and play to our strengths. A 200% profit on $500 is just as significant as a 200% profit on $100,000. It is how clever you are in the hunt (buying and selling). The volume of meat (profits) you bring home is secondary. If possible, start taking action this week, while what I have said is fresh in your mind. If you hesitate, you will probably still be talking about my suggestions a year from now and will have missed current opportunities. You have your whole life ahead of you, so seek out some advice from this book, or some adult you respect, who will take what savings you have and make an investment that is as speculative or conservative as you can handle. You don't want to be foolish and throw the money away on a gamble at the track or the casino, but you can talk to someone in a business that appears to be successful and ask him or her how you can turn your $500 into $1500 within 3 years.

You "survive" by working 12 hours per day.
You "become wealthy" by letting money make money.

Right now, with inflation just beginning to rear its ugly head, you might consider doubling or tripling your present bank savings by buying gold or silver coins. Inflation is a word or concept most people do not understand or appreciate. For your purposes, it is when you compare your part time pay today to the part time pay you will make three years from now. On the upside, you get $8.00 per hour now and three years from now the same part time job will pay about $20.00 per hour. The downside is a movie ticket will then cost you $25.00 and a new pair of jeans $330.00 instead of today's comparatively lower prices. If your money just sits in the bank, it loses purchasing power each year as prices go up and your money stays the same.

Consider looking up the address of a coin shop in your neighborhood, and when you're there let the owner educate you as to how to protect your $500 while at the same time possibly doubling or tripling your money over the next few years. Consider having an adult show you how to open up a stock account with a stockbroker. Look at a gold or silver stock in the range of a dollar or higher. One stock that has my interest is a company that explores for gold and silver. Allegedly, in 2001 they discovered the largest gold deposit in Alaska and the second largest copper mine in the world 16 miles away from Iliamna, Alaska near Bristol Bay. Look it up on a map. Details are in the reference section in this book. I added additional common stock examples, (not recommendations) that I think will increase 300-400% over the next few years, in the reference section, for you to look up and follow just to see how right or wrong I was.

Just Like In The Old Western Movies

The following is an example of how you might let your uninhibited imagination run just to see where it takes you.

If the company's (mentioned above) mining license ever gets Alaska State approval over local environmentalist's objections, then, over the next five years, my guess is, the gold mining company will be spending upwards of $3 billion dollars in equipment to open the mine and build an approximate 80 mile road to the seaport for shipment. They will also be hiring 2000 miners and office staff. They will need houses and shop buildings for a town in a remote wilderness area.

If you own a few shares of the stock at the time, and you apply for a job at their Vancouver, Canada office, you could mention that fact to the person doing the hiring. This will go a long way to assure you a top job for your skill level. You may even like the frontier environment, which will demand wearing a holster and pistol once you're off the campsite or if you go for a swim in the local river. On the down side, the bears and mountain lions will be your neighbors and the snow will be eight feet deep during a long dark winter. On the up side, you will have an adventure to remember the rest of your life. You will have done what other men or women only talk about doing. With 2000 new residents you have limitless new opportunities. You could try being a part time Realtor, homebuilder, restaurateur or the owner of a sporting goods store, childcare center, and more, all before you are 26 years old. By doing any of these, you could make a handsome self-employment profit just working extra hours on the weekends for yourself. In comparison to hanging around your hometown wondering why you're not going anywhere financially, you will be able to save a fairly large sum of money in the local Alaskan bank because the pay scale is almost twice as high in Alaska and there won't be anywhere to spend it! (The reason the pay scale is higher is the sacrifice you make by being in a frontier environment with limited goods, and services.) Take lots of books to read with a flashlight because there is not much else to do after it gets dark. You might even do a little panning for gold on your day off to supplement your income.

Once you have invested a few years of time in Alaska, you may have sufficient saving, or if the stock you bought in the gold mining company has greatly increased in value, you can sell your stock and quit your job. You can then take the cash and make your first independent investment in land, a bush airplane, a hunting or fishing lodge, a jewelry store in your hometown, or what ever appeals to you.

Notes

Chapter 3
"THE PRACTICAL STUFF"

"It is never too late to be what you might have been. This will gratify some and astonish the rest."
Anonymous

Your First Full Time Job

If the Alaskan idea does not appeal to you, let's leave the subject of savings and romance of the frontier and determine how you're going to make some money in this world once you lose mom and dad's warm and fuzzy board and room. The hardest part is finding your first job in high school or after college. Most high schools have a "Career Day." There you will hear adults telling you about how they earn a living doing whatever it is they do - good intentions, but frequently boring. If the speaker would just ask the students what it is they want to hear about before they drone on for a half-hour, maybe everyone would get something out of it.

On Career Day, when I stand before students, I put a great deal of effort into getting the students to tell me something that is currently happening on campus and has everyone's attention before I even mention what I intend to talk about. If I don't get the students to start telling me what they think is important about their life today on campus, then I am wasting their time and mine by describing what I do for a living. Who cares what I do for living? It is only important what the student has in mind, if anything, at that moment. If they tell me what is important to them, then I can relate what I have to say to that subject. Since I do not have the luxury of hearing your views, I have to take a shot at what might appeal to you about getting your first job. Since you need a job to get some experience before you can become a millionaire, it is appropriate we address a sensible way to get you hired over other candidates for the job.

Clothes

I will touch on several important points to help you gain respect from the person interviewing you for a job. The most important consideration is what you wear. Since strangers interviewing you will go with their "first impression."

Choosing what you wear to that interview has to be done carefully. It is the same as when you see a new kid in the school hall and immediately form an opinion as to whether they are a geek or a winner. Keep in mind each society has a dress code ranging from bright colors with lots of body tattoos, to three-piece suits with white shirts and a red tie. These are just beliefs, but if you don't dress according to the tribe you are visiting you will not be accepted.

Think of your clothes as a costume. Think of the job interviewer's office as a stage. The job interviewer is the audience and you are the actor. If you walk in wearing a colored shirt and gym shoes while the present employees all wear white shirts and shined shoes, you will not even come close to getting the job. The reason is the same reason the football team at high school all wear the same uniform. It means you, as team player, are willing to put work rules above the dress code demanded by your friends outside of the work place. Look around you in you classroom or lunchroom. Everyone sitting at a certain table has almost the same costume, hairstyle and make up. If anyone in that group decided to wear a different costume they would have to eat at another table where they were accepted as part of that separate and different tribe.

To find out what to wear to a job interview, do a little investigation by making a phone call to the company you are going to visit. Consider being blunt and ask the receptionist who answers the phone, "Could you tell me what the department managers wear to work each day? I am applying for a job and am coming in for a interview and want to look sharp." If that does not work, then ask someone older, whom you respect, what they would recommend.

Let's assume it is an office job requiring a white shirt, shined shoes, pants that are pressed and a belt to hold up the pants at your waist, versus the current style of wearing pants off the hip. You borrow as many clothes as your older sister or brother has in the closet to meet the menu. After the interview you find you did not get the job. What do you do now? Most of you will just walk away embarrassed. What would you think of the idea of calling the interviewer back and asking him or her what they found in the person they hired that caused that person to be chosen over yourself? Consider asking the interviewer how you could have been better prepared for the interview. When you say good-bye mention you would like to be called for a second interview if the new person does not work out, or another position becomes available.

For someone in your age group to be so forward and confident in themselves would be a most unusual event in the life of the interviewer. The interviewer will suddenly see you as more than "just another kid looking for a job," and there is a strong possibility the interviewer will remember you since you now stand out above the crowd. All employers want to hire people who have some snap to them. Even you want to be with friends who have a sense of adventure and who speak up. You wouldn't hang with someone who is timid or depressing to be with so don't let yourself be depressed just because you were turned down on your first venture. In the movies, all of us like to see the underdog speak up against the establishment. The establishment likes to see this since these are the kind of employees that can help establishment make money. The timid ones are scared of being criticized so they keep their mouths shut and don't have the courage to speak up for change or to suggest improvement for the work place.

Let's talk more about clothes. The costume you're wearing right now is your choice because your friends are wearing the same thing. You should stay with those clothes when you're with them, but to influence strangers or customers to give or pay you money, you need to make a favorable impression so they emotionally trust you. In general, the best-dressed people are the most respected ones in any crowd. All of us physically shrink a little as they pass by if our dress is more casual. Observe that in a crowd those watching the best-dressed walk by actually bow their heads out of respect. If you watch the Oscars Show each year you can see examples of the public actually lowering their heads as the well-dressed women walk bye.

We might even feel a little jealous and angry we can't dress so well, but we still step aside, or submit to their apparent authority just because of their costume. What this means is that each of you has to start thinking about what costume you can financially afford so that you can appear successful. The benefit of this "dress up" approach is most people will assume you are bright, clever, and maybe wealthy. This means a job interviewer will treat you more like a serious job candidate instead of just another inexperienced kid whom he or she wants to get rid of as quickly as possible.

The job interviewer knows what the boss wears to work each day. If you dress like the boss there is an automatic connection in the mind of the interviewer that you and the boss are from the same tribe. He or she as an interviewer had better be careful not to offend you. Maybe the interviewer will unconsciously reason that he or she is protecting his or her job by hiring someone whom the boss notices as dressing like the boss. Maybe the boss will even compliment the job interviewer for selecting a trainee that "fits right in." This translates into a potential raise or bonus for the job interviewer.

In the reference section of this book I mention a book entitled "Dress for Success." I used this as my guide when I first got started, and you should consider getting a copy to study with the same enthusiasm as you might if it was the latest edition of People Magazine. If you can't find a new one, go to the Internet for a used one at half the price.

How Not To Get Hired

The job interviewer is probably just a nice person who has a family and children your age. They will want to hire guys and gals your age who match what they would like for their own children in terms of appearance and behavior. If the appearance you bring to the interviewing table is extreme in any way, you're going to be fighting an uphill battle during the entire interview. Please understand I am not "talking down to you" it is just my way of saying what has to be said.

I will mention some of the gross errors most kids make because no one told them beforehand what would turn off the interviewer:

- **Excessively chewed fingernails.** (If this is a nervous habit and there is no time to grow them out, explain to the interviewer that you are trying to break the habit. This will be a big plus for you since it will show courage and awareness. Remember, the interviewer may have had the same problem when he or she was your age.)
- **Unnaturally colored nail polish** such as black, green, blue, etc.
- **Dirt under the fingernails.**
- **Any unexplainable ornaments** in the skin, tattoos or piercing.
- **Any noticeable overly strong fragrances** both from perfume, cologne or body odor.
- **Shoes that are not shined.**
- **Pants worn off the hip.**
- **Anything sexy** such as cleavage, navel exposure, and pants that are extra tight in the crotch.
- **Unnatural, loud tinted streaks in the hair,** i.e., blue, purple, glitter, etc.

- **Hair that is cut or styled in an extreme way.**
- **Clothing that fits poorly,** is ripped, dirty or not ironed.

On the subject of you looking for your first official job, I came across an entertaining article in Reader's Digest (Sept 2009 Issue page 110) having to do with resumes. It seemed appropriate for teenagers to avoid classic mistakes. Have a laugh and then remember it when you fill out your first Resume. See if you pick up on the irony of the authors that follow:

Employment History:
Last Job - "Restaurant manger. Cleaned and supervised employees."
Job before that- "CFO for a wholesaler of women's slacks. We also sold men's bottoms."
Job before that - "Bum. Abandoned belongings and lead nomadic lifestyle."

References:
"My friend Scott"
"My girlfriend"
" None, I've left a path of destruction behind me"

Interests:
"Gossiping"
"Sex"

Skills:
"Fluent in both English and Spinach"
"Excellent memory, strong math aptitude, and strong memory."

"I can type withoutlookingat the keyk board"
"Able to whistle while pretending to drink water at the same time."

Education:
"Moron University"
"Attended collage courses"

Academic achievement:
"Received the Smith Schlorship Award for Excelence in English"

You have to judge for yourself, but it would be good to bounce your appearance off of some adult before you leave the house for the interview. In general, if you dress and look clean and neat, it will all work out just fine. Essentially, your appearance broadcasts your willingness to accept authority and submit to the rules of the corporate structure. This is another way of telling the world that you're not going to be a troublemaker once you've been hired.

Paying For Your Costume

Now, how does someone without a lot of money pay for those nice expensive clothes? The answer is, "You don't." Look up the local resale shop in the phone book or on the Internet. It will be run by volunteers from some hospital or church type entity. They will collect high quality clothes from rich people who wear things a few times, then discard them as a tax deduction when they are too small to fit an ever-expanding waistline, or are no longer fashionable. The resale shop will often sell a $1000 suit that has been worn only 10 times for $20. They even clean and press the suit before putting it on the rack. The millionaire who donated the suit deducted $200 off of his or her taxes for the donation so it is a win - win situation. A few years after you are fully-grown you can think of new clothes at full price. No sense in putting out a lot of money for clothes when you are still growing.

When you're 25 or so years old, you can think of a new tailor made suit and shirts made in the Orient at one half the retail price here in the States. Just look under "tailors" in the Internet or Yellow pages.

In the reference section I put the phone number of one tailor who travels to large metropolitan cities over the entire USA on a monthly basis to measure customers. We met in the early 1960s when he had just arrived from India and he has dressed my entire family since that time.

Notes

Chapter 4
"YOUR PERSONAL CHOICES"

*"The Golden Rule - Who Ever has
the Gold makes the rules"*

Taking or Giving Orders

The main thought I want to implant in your memory today is that...

Very few people become wealthy working for someone else!

(However, when one is first starting out it's often necessary, to learn how a particular business works so you know what the rules are for success in that business.)

By far the most powerful tool that you have in controlling your future is, and always has been, your ability to discipline yourself. This is the true determining factor of how successful you will be in every area of your life. As you get into your junior or senior year consider the consequences of such things as smoking, doing drugs, or drinking - all of these things will prevent you from saving money. I am not passing judgment on your personal preferences. However, if you insist on spending money on things that disappear in a matter of minutes, (spending $200 for fireworks for the Fourth of July is really watching your savings go up in smoke) you will be dragging a big weight along with you on your road to financial success.

Have you ever given any thought to the cost per week for tobacco, drugs or alcohol? I'll bet the cost is over $50.00 per week. In that case, you're talking about $2000-$3000.00

per year. If you had invested $1000 of that amount instead of spending it and it tripled over 3-5 years, you could end up with a foundation upon which to build your empire. This whole concept is easier said than done. You can still go out and do fun and exciting things to experience life all around you, but consider just starting to use your brainpower to disciple yourself.

Here's a challenge you may want to try for a week or two to test your outer limits. Try depositing in a box on your dresser top an exact duplicate of the amount you spend in cigarettes or other habits, each day. You will be surprised at how much you save. Not only will you profit monetarily, but you will also reach the ultimate human high of being "in control" of yourself. You will have the self-satisfaction in knowing that there isn't any monetary challenge out there that you can't conquer. Once you see how strong you are in the art of self-discipline, making a fortune in money will be an everyday accomplishment. Even if you are not "turned on" to a career of being wealthy after reading this book, the money will be there when you choose to buy that first auto or motorcycle.

A recent, 19-year-old, female graduate has told me that she was able to buy her new boots, some minor designer clothing and travel to Florida for spring break with the money she saved during her junior and senior year. The young lady is not interested in becoming a millionaire from investing (She would rather go the "marry a rich guy" route.) but she earned the right to spend because she disciplined herself to save.

Many of you may find high school boring, but if you keep in mind this concept of seeing yourself as a person that is worthwhile, and continue to challenge yourself, you will never find yourself bored. You will always be striving to better yourself. This is what I'm trying to impart to you, if you have confidence in yourself, you can overcome any challenge. You will succeed in all phases of your life. You will naturally become very wealthy. Those of you who can discipline yourselves will end up with more than adequate money. The result of your self discipline will be that in all probability your future spouse will probably stay with you long enough to celebrate your 50th wedding anniversary because you avoided the divorce court by not having arguments over lack of money. Your children will have respect for you because they will see the respect you have for yourself. Your children will then not give you a hard time, the way some of you might be giving your parents a hard time right now.

Keep in mind that one of the reasons why you may have trouble disciplining yourself could be because your parents can't discipline themselves. All of us want to be "just like dad" or "just like mom". They are our role models. If your environment at home is filled with uncertainty - everyone yelling at the other one, second hand smoke and empty beer cans all over the house - you will probably end up creating the same atmosphere when you have your own home.

On the other hand, if mom and dad are right down the center and you are the loud mouth wise guy in the family, selfish and disorganized, and then consider the following, either you see:

One - *There is nothing out there to fear and you are entitled to become organized and efficient.*

or,

Two - You continue to refuse to follow the rules of organized society and you will end up as an adult on the bottom of the food chain.

This is serious business and you have to make a decision now or you will always be taking orders from someone because you did not save any money. You won't have a choice. Visualize how infuriating it could be to have a future of being " told what to do" all the time. Use this as your driving force to accumulate knowledge and or money. Even if you're not interested in being a millionaire, consider being the most knowledgeable person in your chosen field so you can give the orders instead of having no choice but to take orders from a superior.

Being Your Own Person

If you have an aggravating atmosphere at home now, consider not following in those footsteps when you leave home after high school. To change, you have to understand that you are entitled to a peaceful adulthood. You are not responsible for the unacceptable habits of people you grew up with. Mom and Dad will still love you when you become more successful than they ever thought you could. Even if they try to discourage you from being more than they were, you have to have the strength to brush that talk off and run your own race the way you think it should be run.

All of us have a tape recorder in our heads from the day we are born. Whatever we were taught or whatever impression Mom and Dad or some other joyful or depressing experience put on that tape recorder when we were very, very young is the way we will direct our lives. Our past is what we use to navigate the future. If you find yourself continually irritating other people you need to adjust your viewpoint to the way society will accept you. If your view of how to compromise with others is to scream and rage then there is room for improvement in your viewpoint. None of us can change 100%, but each of us can modify our viewpoint and have a more satisfying adult experience as we grow up.

There is no sense in making your home environment an excuse for being a financial failure. Try to realize that the only important moment in your entire human experience is what happens in the next 5 minutes and the rest of today. What happened earlier today or yesterday is over. It can't be changed.

It is up to you to look in the mirror and give yourself permission to become what you think you should be. If you have a negative background at home, the only way to stop the tape recorder (CD, DVD - in your language) in your head from controlling you is to look in the mirror and say *&# you society! You're not going to keep me from developing to my full potential." If you are too timid to look in the mirror and say something like this, you're probably going to end up living from paycheck to paycheck with some minor job success. If you have a younger brother or sister you care about, you would probably be inclined to encourage them to "Be the best you can be." How about you doing the same thing for yourself

Forgive Yourself

Not feeling guilty about the past is important. Fortunately, you guys are too young to be burdened with a lot of guilt over having done ugly things to other people. Over the next years, however, some of you will drive while drunk, and will crash a car and possibly injure or kill your passenger, yourself or some 10-year-old on a bike. Some of you will say or do something stupid to just the wrong person at the wrong time. Some of you will think you are clever and try to deal drugs or do something else illegal that you will regret for the rest of your life. Fortunately, the large majority of you will never have to deal with such undesirable matters because of the way your parents have brought you up. It could be that you are one of the rare people who were born with a quality that is so stable you can "feel" when the reward is not worth the risk.

I am not here to preach to any of you about morals, or premeditated harm you might do to other humans. The courts of law will massage you with steel wool for willfully hurting some other person. My concern is the everyday unintentional accidents or negligence that could have been avoided. But, it happened and now you have to deal with your mistake. I want to give you a formula on how to handle the situation since all of us have had this undesirable experience and we can't change yesterday.

Mistake... When it happens, you have a choice of either going into a depression, where you walk around in a stupor until the shock wears off, or you can forgive yourself instantly. You can't change what happened 30 seconds ago or yesterday. However, you can forgive yourself on the grounds you did not intend to make the mistake. You need to take responsibility for your mistake and provide restitution or apologize. If you want to temporarily wallow in blame and shame that is permissible. What you can't do if you want to become a millionaire is to start in on yourself with self-punishment to try to suffer yourself clean. Mutilating your own body does not repair the body of your victim. Just stay cool and do what ever is necessary to ease the pain of the person you accidentally hurt.

   Self-punishment is where you feel guilty and find ways to hurt yourself by saying or doing just the wrong thing every day. It takes a really strong person to forgive him or herself. I am not talking about brushing the ugly event off and pretending it never happened. You have to deal with the truth and seek forgiveness from the other party you injured, but also, realize that you can't change yesterday. You have to pick up the pieces and move on as best you can. You want to avoid being one of those people in an asylum who is there because they insist on trying to change yesterday. Since they can't reverse the ugly "instant replay" that keeps playing over and over in their mind, they turn inward on themselves from guilt or disappointment and drift off into a silent world of their own.

   The other side of the coin is to forgive the other person who has hurt you physically or emotionally. This is very, very difficult to do. Until you forgive both yourself and the other fellow you really can't move forward. Dragging along the weight of non-forgiveness is just too heavy a load as you climb the mountain towards becoming a millionaire.

In your own family, look at the constant misery one member might be suffering because they are still talking about some insult or negligence to or from a 3rd party that happened years ago. Consider suggesting to that person just what I said about their forgiving either the other fellow or their own unpremeditated mistakes. You will feel good about yourself for having addressed the issue in an effort to "help someone else," and you will reward yourself accordingly.

Premeditated attacks on others are outside of the "mistake" category and frequently the only relief is when the victim forgives you. If the victim is unavailable then you had better seek Professional advice to find out why you planned to hurt the other person in the first place.

Not allowing yourself to become depressed over some shocking event in your future life is a lot easier to talk about than to do. It is important you understand how depression works so you realize how it will keep you in poverty until you snap out of it. If you are at least aware of the basics, you might be able to see yourself or one of your friends starting to go downhill, and maybe turn yourself or them around because you have a minimal understanding of what is happening to either of you.

The following is what the college Psychology textbooks say happens when you go into a depression. Typically, you go into a state of being numb immediately after the shock of the event. As the shock wears off in a week or so, you may start thinking of suicide for yourself, because of guilt. If you get through that period you are extremely angry with yourself and if you get through that period you are then angry with everyone around you. By then no one wants to live with you and you are probably into alcohol, drugs, or live as a homeless person in a cardboard box under a highway. This is not something you want to drift into because of some unacceptable event you may or may not have been able to prevent.

I am not saying such an extreme mental breakdown occurs every time you screw up, or your pet goldfish goes belly up, but a typical example for the guys is when you drop the potential winning touchdown pass, or strike out with the bases full. You just want to die on the spot. For the girls, an example is a fall on the ice during a figure skating competition or a slip on the parallel bars after so many, many hours of practice. Every coach has made the same mistakes on their way up. Forgive yourself and move on. If the other girls in the audience could skate even close to your skill level they would be on the ice instead of being spectators.

Watch television and see how the pros react when they make a mistake. They brush it off since it is "over" and they can't change it. The highly skilled baseball player gets paid a great deal to get on base one out of every three times at the plate for a 333. Average.

During the Olympics, the skater who commits a minor error might go to 3rd place. Sometimes third place becomes, 1st or 2nd if the skaters in 1st or 2nd fall. Remember, it is never over until the final bell rings. Consider never "giving up" out of shame or guilt. There are times to quit when you are injured or outmatched by a superior force and when giving up is good judgment.

Consider giving 100% until the final bell so your opponent will remember you with respect.

Money Reserve

Many millionaires have committed suicide when their business suddenly failed. They could not accept the thought of going back to working for an hourly wage when they were used to treating $100 bills as pocket change. For those of you who do become millionaires, condition yourself at an early time to have emergency money reserves, which you do not touch no matter what. This reserve will help you to stay cool and probably save you from jumping off of your penthouse condo outdoor deck on the 38th floor because you have lost everything from some investment that went sour. It is never over. You can come back the same way you made your first million. It will take 4- 5 more years to rebuild, but you can do it. Having some emergency money stashed away will give you a foundation for your next move up. If depression comes your way seek advice from a professional or find forgiveness from someone.

Have Some One Else Pay Your College Tuition

Let's move to a lighter subject. How can you help your parents reduce the cost of your college tuition? Starting this summer, consider saving money to show dad that you are trying to keep his potential college costs down. Maybe he will be open to matching your savings. That way, at time of high school graduation, he does not have to think about "the proper gift" for you. It is a win-win situation since dad gets to keep the money if you don't go to college and you will bust your rear end to make sure you succeed in getting accepted at the college of your choice. The two of you can have a good laugh over the competition. Dad and mom will be increasingly proud of you since you honored them by letting them be part of your preparation for the your future college experience. It could be a bonding experience where all of you become equals versus the parent/child relationship you have now.

There are the usual ways you have all heard about regarding academic scholarships. However, there is another non-scholastic scholarship you might consider. I realize I am now addressing a very limited teenage audience, on this particular awareness message, but if one or two of you pick up on my suggestion, it makes it worthwhile using up the space in this book to pass on the information. The Scholarship is called the Chick Evan's Caddie Scholarship. I enrolled at the University of Wisconsin on this scholarship back in 1954. It is specifically for caddies at private golf courses who are in the upper portion of their class, have caddied for 2 seasons at a private club in the area where they live, and have parents with low to average income.

There is no quota from each golf course. A single course can recommend 1 or 10 male or female caddies each year. Now listen to this. It pays all your tuition, board and some of the larger fees from the University. The only thing you have to do is feed yourself. This can be done easily by getting a job as a waiter or waitress at the local fraternity or sorority house during meal hours. If you want to top this off with a 10 hour per week job at the local bar, you will have enough spending money to really enjoy University events. Mom and dad can go to Italy or Costa Rica for a vacation instead of having to sacrifice to send you to school. You will be saving them over $20,000 per year by doing this. If you are in Illinois you can go to Northwestern and not pay the $45,000 per year tuition.

You could be one of the few students who end up with more money in his or her bank account at the end of college than when you first enrolled. This then opens the door after college to invest in something like run down real estate, which you then fix up and sell at a profit - your first real stride forward in becoming a millionaire. The phone number to call for information on this caddie scholarship is in the reference section at the back of this book under Western Golf Associations, Golf, Illinois.

Besides the scholarship aspect, a caddie can earn $75 a day most of the time for 5 hours of carrying a golf bag. Being outdoors and meeting other guys and gals your own age who are generally into athletics and clear thinking. Some of the current star golf pros were introduced to golf as caddies. If you are interested in golf and dad does not belong to a private club, you probably can't afford to pay the high cost to play golf, so caddying gives you the opportunity for finding out if you could ever become a professional golfer. At the same time, there is a good chance of your getting free golf lessons from the club pro if he happens to like you. It is a win-win situation.

Another perk is that frequently you bond with a member at the club who sees you as the son or daughter he or she would have liked to have had, but it did not work out. As a result, you get semi-adopted and this member becomes your mentor or guide to your first job out of high school or college.

In Your Own Neighborhood

If you just can't get to a golf course in your area, consider some of the many ways to make self employed income when you're not in school. One example that impressed me was a mother's story about her 12 year old, who took a small children's wagon with 3 plastic bags of planting soil and went from house to house in the spring finding neighbors who wanted him to plant their small vegetable gardens with seeds he bought from a catalogue. He ended up earning as much as $95 in a single day.

Speaking of coincidences, this same individual is sitting in my office this very minute since I hired him last Friday as a loan officer trainee for the mortgage business. He is now 21 years old and his first job is to proofread the manuscript that made up the final edit that I am typing today. This book goes to the printer tomorrow. He just now asked me to mention to all of you readers that during his teens he went around with his push-power mower in his suburban neighborhood during the summer and made over $3000 each summer. He highly recommends this as a way to earn cash and plan your own hours. Now this is the kind of guy everyone wants to hire! Consider putting that sort of experience on any resumes you send out and elaborate on it. It shows you are special and not just ordinary.

Here are a few other ideas:

1. You can justify buying an auto if you use it to make money - for example, being on call for picking up and delivering for older people in retirement homes.

2. You can paint houses or fences.

3. You can wash windows.

4. You can mend or sew peoples clothing at their house.

5. Power washing - Another way to make some serious money is to go around the neighborhood power washing auto engines under the hood or blasting old peeling paint off old garages or outdoor decks. Even at age 16 you can handle the equipment. Have Dad buy you a lightweight 1400 psi power sprayer at one of the local hardware stores for $100.00. You can even buy one on e-bay. Dad will show you how to handle it safely and you can practice blasting paint off of old boards around the house. Then roll it down the street in your neighborhood. It has luggage like features with the handle and the two wheels for easy of rolling it behind you. All you do is hook it up to the customer's garden hose, aim and pull the trigger. You girls can do this also, because it is a lightweight unit. It is important that you wear safety glasses since the fragments from the object being cleaned will be flying in a thousand directions and you really have to protect your eyes.

Also, find a home in an expensive neighborhood that has bricks (called PAVERS) with weeds or moss growing between them or a driveway of black asphalt that has cracks. Knock on the door and ask if they want you to clean the driveway so it will look like new again. With your maximum spray power you can blast the dirt and growth out in a minimum of time and really make the driveway look like new. You will get fine dirt all over your clothes, your face and your hair (very important you wear SAFETY GLASSES). You might consider wearing outer clothes over your T-shirt and Jeans since you will need to remove the outer clothes and put them in the trunk before getting back in your car.

Charge them $25.00 per hour and you will pay for the equipment Dad bought you in two days. Once the neighbors trust you they will call you to clean all sorts of things and you may have to hire some of your friends. Think of the excitement of having serious cash in your pocket and a feeling of independence. If you want to earn $50.00 per hour then ask the homeowner if they want you to fill in the area between the bricks or in the cracks on the asphalt with sand that has an epoxy in it. After you put a light spray of water on the sand it starts to harden to almost solid concrete and that prevents weeds or moss from growing on the pavers or asphalt. You can buy the paver sand at a store like Home Depot or Menards for a modest price. The reason you can charge more is that you own the sand. On the lighter side - maybe this experience will be so enjoyable you will choose Dentistry (love opening and filling those cavities $$$) for a career after graduation from a 4 year University.

On the subject of Dentistry I recently signed up at the University Of Illinois Dental School in Chicago to have students work on several tooth problems I was having. The idea was to experience at least one professional career that involved students so I could give you 17-19 year old readers some insights as to what you will face if you decide to become a professional service provider. Bottom line is that the University of Illinois has such an outstanding reputation that a graduate can expect a starting salary of approximately $110,000.00 per year on his or her first job. The downside is that tuition is $93,000.00 per year. (What would we do without student loans?) A secondary benefit that came to me is that each visit for work on my teeth consumed 3-4 hours. The student and the teachers spent 75% of the time on the education on each of my individual teeth and 25% doing repair work. At first I did not like all the academics and consumption of my time, but the more they educated me about each tooth in my mouth the more I realized what a generous preventive maintenance service the School provides. The fact that their repair charges are 1/3 the cost of the average neighborhood dentist was a welcome surprise.

On the subject of having fun and making the maximum amount of money from the Power Washer even before you graduate from high school, consider getting your Dad to help you build the following in the back yard:

Have Dad buy you from the hardware store:

- Two 8' long 4" x 4" posts
- Two 4' long 4" x 4" posts.
- Clamps or screws to connect them
- One 6' tall clear sheet of Plexiglas. (This can be any width you want. Six feet is adequate)
- At least two pairs of safety glasses.

Instructions

- Attach the saw cut end of one of the 8' posts to the center of one of the 4' posts with a clamp or screws of some kind creating a "T" shape.

- Do the same thing with the other post.

- Turn them upside down so that both of the 4' posts are on the grass with the 8' post sticking straight up in the air.

- Then have Dad attach both posts to the Plexiglas making a 6-foot tall shield (as wide as you want. (6 feet is adequate at this time).

- Cut out one or more holes in the Plexiglas to be able to poke the nozzle of the Power Washer through and also allow you to move 2 inches from side to side of the hole.

You have just created a "Power Washer Target Range".

Invite the kids in the neighborhood over to blast away at what ever targets you put on the other side of the shield - wood, Styrofoam, aluminum cans, etc. Initially, charge them approximately $3.00 for 10 minutes use of the power washer. If there is a great deal of excitement over blasting away at an object to the point of destruction by the kids in the neighborhood, then you can install a second Power Washer through another hole in the Plexiglas and two kids can compete against each other. You can give the winner a small prize.

The shield protects the users from any flying debris. Safety glass must still be worn at all times since "you never know".

If you want to try to sell this concept to a Water Park in a ready made kit that you and Dad construct, then consider having all the targets be frozen water comic book figures with a prize inside of them to hand back to the "shooter". This will eliminate any clean up mess and the water park will have the water on site.

Now, imagine the expansion plans if the idea takes hold. You could rent an indoor retail store and have 10 Power Washers going at once. You could have Dad helping out with a fast food and drink restaurant so the other kids could have a birthday party at the "Water Target Range" you have created. You could show a Bank how much money is coming in and then get a Small Business Loan from the local Bank and open a dozen more Target Ranges in the area.

Dad could quit his job and between the two of you there would be more money coming in than Dad was making before quitting his present job. My Patent lawyer said this idea is too easy to get around so it is not worth the expense of even a limited or restrictive Patent.

If you live near an Industrial Park or an Auto Repair Garage you might walk from shop to shop asking if they would like you to Power Wash the oil and grease off of the floor of the Repair area or the steps leading into the office from the Repair area. They are generally too busy to clean because they have one emergency after the other and you might get 2-3 jobs a day earning $125.00 for 5 hours of work. Also, it is kind of fun to blast away with a Power Washer and get paid on top of it.

In today's market clear profit of $20.00 per hour is a reasonable estimate for what you should expect to get paid when you're running your own business if you are finding the customers. If you have to work for someone then aim at $10.00 per hour since they have all the aggravation of finding the customers.

Now that I have you thinking, consider writing down whatever idea just popped into your head. If you don't write it down it will probably evaporate over the next few seconds.

A very important result of your getting your first single self-employed job is twofold. First, you learn more about how to do something practical and valuable. This new skill can justify your charging more per hour for the same task to your next client. Second, if you did a decent job, you may get the first client to refer you to another neighbor. All you have to do is merely ask your first client whom he or she might recommend you call on who may also need the same service. You then use this same legitimate technique on the second customer in order to get to a third customer. The most important thing is for you to find your first customer. If you can sell a single customer, you can sell a hundred. If you can't get a single customer, then you stop, and try another idea.

For more information and specifics regarding available legal and successful money making methods, and maybe even some entrepreneurial advice, consider going to the library or search the web. Authors have been writing on this subject for a long time. The only disappointment you will experience is the majority of them deal with borrowing money from an adult and going into an aggressive retail business where they allege you will make a quick fortune.

At your age, you have a lot of legitimate teenage priorities having nothing to do with the discipline required for a full-scale business opportunity. Why not just relax and go with the flow for the immediate future once you have read this book. There is not any rush. The thing I am trying to sell you on is to start thinking about this subject and start saving your money. Once you see you can save money, you will feel the spark for investing and it will all come together in your head. Try not to get envious, if you read some newspaper headlines about a teenager who took an idea, created an Internet Web site around that idea, and ended up making millions of dollars from people wanting to advertise on his or her newly created site. On the up side, that rare individual should be honored for stepping up to the plate and fearlessly trying a new adventure. On the downside, that rare individual who takes on the pressure of having to make decisions in an adult business world will have to spend so much time managing the business, that there will not be no time to enjoy the precious junior and senior years of high school.

Freshman and sophomore years are a kind of a holding period for most students, where things are uncertain as we go from childhood to pre-adulthood. The last two years of high school is the time to make lifetime friends, and begin our independence from mom and dad. Imagine yourself as the rare individual who makes a million dollars at age 16. You would be so busy managing 6 employees who might be twice your age and miss the entire excitement of being with your friends for the last two years of high school.

To repeat, honor and give respect to the individual who was so successful with the Internet Web site just the same as you would to the 16 year old who won the Silver Medal in the Olympics, and realize that your day is still to come. Consider the price the successful 16-year-old teenager has had to pay to take on his or her Olympic victory or Internet fame mentioned above. That individual has shed a few tears over having to separate him or herself from friends due to hours and hours of practice. Consider befriending that super successful individual, the same way you might befriend a socially retarded individual on the other end of the spectrum. In both cases they need to be told by their own age group that they are OK even if they don't have the time or capacity to flow with their high school crowd.

If you do what I have suggested you will feel good about yourself. You would have treated those individuals the same way you would have liked to be treated if your time for material success had come early, or if you were born with a mental perceptual handicap where people told jokes and you constantly missed the punch line. Either extreme has its benefits and burdens. You are what you are today and that is good enough for the moment. Once you accept this approach, the joy of feeling good about yourself will cause you to excel in everything that appeals to you, be it the upper limits of your handicap or your natural free flowing talents.

Put your thoughts down in a Journal or on the following Note pages.

Notes

Notes

Chapter 5
"HELPFUL HINTS AS YOU MATURE"
Business Hints

How to make an educated guess on who is honest and hard working and who is undependable, by their facial features.

"You are what you eat" is the theory behind this subject called Macrobiotics. Consider looking this subject up on the Web. This will give you the upper hand when meeting someone for the first time.

You will learn to interpret what you see on a persons face as being a strong or weak quality towards hiring that person for a job you have to offer. You can also look at your own facial features in the mirror. You may decide to change them by changing your diet. The less you contaminate your body with chemicals and sugars the more handsome you as a man will appear to the women, and the more clear skinned and radiant the women will appear to the men.

Just about every book on Macrobiotic has pictures and diagrams of facial features to help you make judgments about people as soon as you meet them. Michio Kushi is an author from Japan who published the first books and pamphlets on this subject in the USA around 1970. His facial diagrams are based on earlier works from 1000 years ago in Japan. Go to the Reference section on page 65-69 in this book for more information

A Few Examples:

1. Look at the eyebrows of the other person.
   If they slant upward the person is more "YANG" and probably very stubborn. However they are organized and get the job done. The Warrior-Type.

   If the eyebrows are slanted downward this person is more "YIN" and is more creative. They are probably interested in art, crafts, cooking and are conscious of their environment and nature. They are fun to be with, tend to be very enthusiastic and talk a lot, but don't always follow through with action. The Nurturing-Type.

   Most of us have flat eyebrows and you can't make a judgment one way or another. Consider picking out one of the kids at school who is the leader of the group and another one who is all talk but with no action. Then silently observe their facial features.

2. If the other person has a large lower lip that means they may have a weak lower intestine. The Macrobiotic authors say that you should be aware that this hints of a weak or selfish personality.

3. If the other person has a nose that is oversized and has blue or red veins showing, it likely they consume a large quantity of refined sugar such as alcohol, drugs, candy, ice cream, etc. This type of person has problems disciplining themselves so they are more likely to arrive at work late and have such a short attention span they can't complete their assigned tasks.

Many of the books will have diagrams of facial features that exhibit everything from being able to tell who is bordering on being a serial killer to someone who nods their head in agreement when you are talking, but is slightly "perceptually handicapped" and did not grasp the meaning of what you just said.

Another idea is to get a Handwriting analysis. Before you team up with a partner or hire any employee consider spending $25.00 to get a handwriting analysis of the other party. All you need to do is ask them to give you their permission in writing.

Handwriting Analysis: For Years From Now When You Need to Hire Employees

As teenagers I realize this subject may not appeal to you now. However, once you enter the business world it is really expensive to hire someone who has a bad track record and find out the hard way that you should not have hired them. Try to remember the concept at this age so when you're 30 it is a familiar idea.

The way you go about this is to have the other party give you permission in writing. Then you use that permission as the example to send to the Professional Handwriting Expert. You mail the original to a Handwriting Expert (look on the Web) and usually within a day you will get a report. The report will tell you a great deal about what to expect from this person. You can avoid a lot of wasted money hiring someone who is a smooth talker and looks like just the person for the job or partner only to find out he or she has "tendencies" that you need to investigate further. Tendencies might be to lie, to steal or cheat, etc. You can then take these "Red Flags" and dig further into the background of the perspective applicant on those issues.

A good way to understand how accurate these writing tests can be is to spend $25.00 and send in your single paragraph and have an analysis on yourself. The report will probably highlight the majority of your strengths and weaknesses. You will feel good about yourself for the positive comments. On the "room for improvement areas" you can then ask your best friend if he or she sees you as having those shortcomings. It can only help you to make more money if you understand how people see you. You can find "Handwriting Analyst" on the web and it is a good idea to ask for references via email.

Personal Hints: Boy - Girl Relationships

Question: *Why does the girl or boy you are attracted to frustrate you to the point of tears sometimes?*

Answer: They are the exact opposite of you in most all ways and that is what fascinates you about them. Each of you "brings to the table" exactly what the other does not have. Together you make a "whole". You feel complete when you are with each other. The price you pay for this sincere relationship is that you will never "understand" each other.

You are not meant to understand each other. He wants the sports and you want the concert. He wants you to be with him at a noisy singles bar with his school buddies. You want him to take ballroom dancing classes at the local Junior College. There is no end to the aggravation and differences, but without that particular person both of you feel incomplete. Over time you learn to accept the necessary everyday compromises.

Try not to be confused or threatened by this basic difference. As you accept the world around you and go with the flow you will have your share of all the excitement of discovery, starting with your first kiss. Just relax and enjoy the ride.

At the heart of the matter is that with most females... no matter what they have... they want something new and different (boots or clothes). With the males... no matter what they have... they want the same old thing (5 year old washed out sweatshirt). If it weren't for females insistent desire to buy new products for commercial glitter (jewelry) or individual glamour (a new lipstick or extra tight Levi's to attract males) there would be almost zero commercial progress.

Long about the 4th year when selfishness creeps into the relationship then the arguments start. No advice giver can help you on this issue. You are on your own. However, try to remember that the reason for the friction and the lack of understanding between you and your significant other is just that your exact opposites. Once you accept that you are never going to understand each other because you are exact opposites maybe you will calm down and get through the current trauma. All of us that have married have gone through the same thing you are probably experiencing today. When these disappointments begins to happen think about the chicken that never would have come out of the egg if it knew in advance what was its future would be like. Maybe at just the worst moment in the relationship you will remember the chicken comment above and start to laugh. That might trigger an instant halt in the ugly verbal incident and the two of you can have a "light moment" instead of continuing the incident.

You will survive together if what the other person brings to the table is so valuable to you that you allow yourself to accept that your partner has to tolerate you the same as you have to tolerate him or her. Easier said than done, but try to stay cool and discuss what I have just said with the partner. You may end up laughing at each other's faults and the "horrible" problem may mellow down to just ordinary compromise.

I recall hearing someone say in the past that before you marry someone each partner practices the art of Enterprise (wooing the other party), but once you are married whether you like it or not you both end up with the art of Compromise (consider taking a deep breath and letting the other person say what they have to say... maybe you will learn something)

You can make a huge amount of money if you understand these basic differences between males and females.

Do a verbal survey with the females you know on the product you want to sell. Until the female says "yes, I think I would buy that for myself or my boyfriend" don't bother trying to produce it. Something is missing.

Problem Solving Between the Sexes

Look at it this way. **Example:** You have 12 problems in individual boxes on a shelf that have to be dealt with at a particular moment.

The more male (Yang) of the two of you will take the most pressing single problem down off the shelf one at a time. He or she will go as far as they can to correct that problem and then put that box back on the shelf. Then take the 2nd most pressing problem and repeat the process. After that, that person will go off and feel a sense of accomplishment and reward his or herself accordingly.

The other partner who is more Yin (emotional) will take all 12 boxes down at once... try to solve or move forward on all 12 at once... get frustrated and have a good cry... leave the boxes laying scattered on the floor and then go off shopping or to see what the children are doing.

Try to see that this is a "good" thing. If both of you were super efficient then you would be like good friends that you admire but you will never fall in love with. The spark and excitement of being together would be missing. You can't have it both ways. The more male (Yang) of the two of you will take the most pressing single problem down off the shelf one at a time. He or she will go as far as they can to correct that problem and then put that box back on the shelf. Then take the 2nd most pressing problem and repeat the process. After that, that person will go off and feel a sense of accomplishment and reward his or herself accordingly.

The other partner who is more Yin (emotional) will take all 12 boxes down at once... try to solve or move forward on all 12 at once... get frustrated and have a good cry... leave the boxes laying scattered on the floor and then go off shopping or to see what the children are doing.

Try to see that this is a "good" thing. If both of you were super efficient then you would be like good friends that you admire but you will never fall in love with. The spark and excitement of being together would be missing. You can't have it both ways.

Several Rules for the Men *(or the more Yang of the two of you.)*:

Even as a teenager, learn to say, "yes dear and no dear" early on. All a Yin person wants is for you to agree with them at the moment. Once the moment has passed then the more Yang person can evaluate the facts and act on what they think is best for the partnership regardless of what that (Yin) person agreed to 3 minutes earlier.

The Yin person who reads this is likely to be angry with me and may think I am being "chauvinistic". However, this is a natural thing for a Yang person to do in order to move matters to a more sensible conclusion. You will probably observe over time that when the more Yang person does the opposite of what they agreed to do, the Yin person in general will not even notice. The Yin person will be taken up with something new the next day. The probability is that they see the new thing as more super important, and can't even recall what they were so anxious about the day before. To keep the peace all you (as the Yang person) did was to keep your mouth shut and try to understand.

If the Yang person is a male, **try to realize that only a "fool" argues with a girlfriend.** All she has to do is shed a single tear and all of your logical arguments evaporate. All she wants is for you to "actually" listen to what she is saying, even if you don't act on it. Consider just keeping your mouth shut and listening. Maybe you will learn something if you actually listen to what she is trying to express.

Everything I have said is done with sincerity and meant to give both of you something to fall back on when there is disagreement between you. You, as the more Yang of the two partners (male or female) may have to bite your lip to keep from exploding, but the pain of a damaged lip is a small price to pay for not having shouted back at the more Yin partner who verbally keeps coming at you and just won't stop talking. It takes real self-discipline, but as you are the more Yang person, you are stuck with the responsibility of keeping things "calm" and not getting sucked into an argument you can never win.

When you reach the point where she or he is just not worth it any more you can justify the "next step" because you gave the relationship your best shot and it is time for you to move on.

Several Rules for the Women: *(or the more Yin of the two of you.)*

If you want to ruin the relationship all you have to do is "tell" your boyfriend what to do instead of "ask" him.

If you ask him if he will do something for you, you should expect "Ok with me, what ever you want." If you "tell" him to do something then you should expect silence for about 3 seconds and then a semi violent verbal explosion.

The teenage boy is the "Head of the Family" (so to speak) when it comes to making decisions. However, the teenage girl (so to speak) is the "Neck of the Family" and if she can discipline herself to phrase every request on her part in the form of a question then she can turn the Head any direction she wants. (This QUIP is from the movie "My Fat Greek Wedding").

It is not easy for a teenager to be that disciplined, but if you implement this early on in the relationship it will pay handsome dividends in getting 90% of what you want without ever having to raise your voice. If you "ask" him and he still comes back at you with "why are you always asking for things, I will make those decisions", then you should consider neutralizing your relationship.

Two Forks and a Dessert

We all think we KNOW the person we are in enamored with, and we dream we could live with them for the next 60 years, but nothing will show you their true nature more than time.

There is no actual test, but keep your eyes wide open. Who will be the first to eat the last forkful of a delicious dessert? Will your partner gobble up the last luscious piece? Or will they offer the last taste to you? In one act you might find an embedded nature/belief that you didn't think they had. Perhaps one event is not sufficient; you may need a half dozen "desserts" for several months to find out the true beliefs of your partner. These basic beliefs come from childhood and your partner will never change. A selfish person is always going to be selfish. Consider finding a person who puts your satisfaction before their own. Remember it goes both ways, you must always respect, listen and discuss what is best for the both of you when you are in a serious, long-term relationship. If you do this, your marriage will survive many obstacles.

Dealing with a Bully

The following is brought in under Helpful Hints because if you are 15-16 years old and not fully-grown it is really aggravating to be hassled or bullied by some of the older or stronger classmates.

Example: Suppose you are in freshmen or sophomore

year and you are temporarily on the receiving end of a lot of waste matter being dumped on you by some "Bully" at school. You have to protect yourself in whatever human way you can.

To prevent getting injured at the outset by the bully you might need to use an emergency human tool by shouting, "The only reason you are attacking me is to distract all the other kids from seeing how scared you are every day of your life".

Of course you may physically, get pounded by the bully for doing that, but if you survive your first defensive challenge you might then go onto to screaming, "You can beat me up, but what is your father going to do to you when he gets you home after he has to go down to the Police Station to bail you out and pay $1500.00 out of his wallet?"

These responses will probably stop the bully cold, because the father might be coming home drunk several times a week and slapping the bully around just to release his anger from his workday.

The fear of what the father might do after having put out $1500.00 would be terrifying to the bully.

These are a few additional verbal weapons you might use to neutralize a bully before he or she actually attacks you, as follows:

"Look Buddy… just because it will only take you 5-6 years to graduate from High School that doesn't make you better than the rest of us."

"Look Buddy… as smart as you is and as dumb as I am, I am still smarter than you are as dumb as I am".

"Look Buddy… if you continue to fool around and fool around you may go home crying".

"Look Buddy… If you hurt me, then just wait until your Mother hears about it and takes away your allowance or your Barbie Doll."

This human approach to your immediate problem is very sensible and the threat may end there. However, you may need a different approach, which requires a good pair of running shoes. If you find a graceful retreat at top speed is necessary then go for it and do not look back.

It could be that the bully acts like a tough guy or gal so you won't see how scared, frightened and uncertain he or she is for any number of reasons. It is all a cover-up. The bully is just angry with everyone. Since you are smaller, he or she sees you as an easy target.

Police Record

Have you ever heard any of your friends claim…."I didn't think I was doing anything wrong" when they ended up getting arrested? That is what the Police hear most often at time of arrest. Years ago the Teenagers were brought home when they were arrested for breaking the law and the father punished the Teenager with a whipping from his leather belt. The Police thought that was good enough. *It was an insult to the entire family to have someone embarrasses the family name by breaking the law.*

Nowadays, some Teenagers want absolute freedom to do whatever they want whenever they feel like it. Consider not getting in with the crazy ones at High School. You most likely will always be living from pay check to pay check when you have a stain on your honesty record. No one will take you under their wing to teach you anything. To avoid the punishment of breaking the Law, how about you and I agreeing right this minute on **playing a Game** to side step your ever needing to break the law just to get money for Concerts, buying a car and other legitimate needs.

The rules of the game are that you collect as many dollar bills as you can, from legal sources, into your top drawer of the Dresser in your room (I mention this in a earlier section of the book) for the next 30 days. Count them. Now repeat for the next 30 days. Now compare the two totals. If you see a gain in the 2nd month over the first 30 days, then for the first time in your young life you will have used your brain and not your physical body to accomplish something. You will be proud of yourself. It will be YOU who decided to play the game. YOU who decided what the rules of the game would be. YOU who set the timetable for measuring success or failure. YOU who just laid your own future financial foundation. Logically, you will have greater self-respect. You will have greater self-confidence. You will see that if you can succeed in this simple Game with the dresser drawer...... then there is not a single money challenge in all of your future human existence that you can't conquer.

When you are approximately 35 years old you may have more money in the bank than you ever thought possible. You will probably look back at this Game with the top dresser drawer as being the cause of your success. The reason is that you will use this same pattern (same as a pattern in Karate training) of having more money next month than you had last month as a normal monthly goal. It won't even be a big deal. You will find ways to make it happen. Setbacks will occur, but you will ride them out the same as riding out a heavy rainstorm. Soon as the storm passes you will merely pick up the pieces and start in again. If you remember the Sylvester Stallone "ROCKY" movies then you know what I am talking about.

Sexting, Texting & Criminal Acts

When you are young you have so many paths to choose. You can do anything with your life. Teacher, Banker, Attorney, Senator, even President - but one mistake, in one instant can make many of those paths disappear from your life horizon.

One charge of sexting, one possession charge, one drinking and driving or texting while driving can ruin your and even your families life for ALL or many years to come.

Here are the Facts: *All of these legal facts below for Sexting, Possession of a Controlled Substance and Texting While Driving are taken from www.legalmatch.com, verbatim.*

3 Ways to Try Juveniles as Adults: There are three common ways in which to transfer a case from juvenile court to the adult system and try the juvenile as an adult. These are:

- **Judicial Waiver** - some states give juvenile court judges the power to have a juvenile's case tried in adult criminal court

- **Direct File** - sometimes called "Prosecutorial Discretion" - some states give prosecutors the power to decide whether or not a juvenile will be tried as an adult

- **Statutory Exclusion** - some states have laws that require a youth's case to be tried in adult court - these laws usually base this automatic transfer on the youth's age, the seriousness or type of crime, and the juvenile's prior record

- **Reverse Waiver** - In a few cases, such as murder or rape, the assumption is that a juvenile should be tried as an adult unless the trial court rules that the case should be sent to juvenile court.

- **Once An Adult, Always An Adult** - In some states, if a juvenile is tried once as an adult, than the juvenile will be tried as an adult in all subsequent cases.

SEXTING:

What is sexting? Sexting is defined as the act of transmitting sexually explicit messages, primarily through the use of cell phone text messaging. The messages usually contain illicit photographs or video links depicting the person sending them. They can be sent from one person to another, and sometimes they may be sent to mass recipients.

Sexting is a growing trend primarily amongst teenagers who send "sext" messages in connection with dating or flirting. The main concern is that if the person sending or receiving the message is under the legal age of adulthood, they may be convicted of possession or distribution of child pornography (especially if the photograph depicts a minor).

Sexting can also create major problems if the explicit pictures are obtained by other persons without the sender's consent, such as an older person or a registered sex offender. Sexting is a relatively recent development, so the laws governing it are sometimes still in development and may vary from state to state.

What states are prosecuting sexting charges? Many states impose criminal penalties for sexting. This is usually done under the umbrella of child pornography laws. Sexting is specifically illegal in several states, and at least 20 others are considering criminalizing the act. Some states that are known to prosecute for sexting charges include Indiana, New York, Ohio, Pennsylvania, Virginia, and Wyoming.

What types of sentencing are involved in sexting charges? Depending on the jurisdiction's sexting laws, sexting can result in either felony or misdemeanor criminal charges.

Sentencing for felony charges can result in heavy fines from $500-$1,000 and/or a prison sentence of at least one year. Misdemeanor charges result in fines of hundreds of dollars and/or one year maximum in jail.

Again, the main concern in sexting sentences is whether child pornography laws apply. Such laws are where the state derives their authority to impose felony charges for the act of sexting. Child pornography charges in a sexting context can also result in the defendant being placed on a registered sex offender list. In some states even minors have been placed on such lists as a result of sexting charges.

Possession:
What is Constructive Possession of a Controlled Substance? Constructive possession of a controlled substance exists where you do not have actual physical possession of an illegal drug, but have both:

- **knowledge** of the drug's presence on or about your property and the ability to **maintain dominion and control over it.**

Constructive possession can be sole or joint, meaning either an individual or a group of two or more people can be charged with constructively possessing the same controlled substance. For example, two people living in the same house where only one bag of marijuana is found can both be held liable for constructively possessing the single bag.

Merely being in close proximity to a drug is not enough to prove constructive possession. Legally, it is treated the same as actual possession and allows for the same possible defenses.

What is Considered "Knowledge"? Although laws differ from state to state, generally, knowledge has two components:

- You must know that the substance is on or around your property. This knowledge does not have to be actual, but can be inferred from incriminating facts or circumstances.

- You must know or should have known of the illegal nature of the drug.

What is Considered the "Ability to Maintain Dominion and Control"? The ability to maintain dominion and control has been interpreted differently by almost every jurisdiction in the United States and the meaning often changes from case to case. Generally speaking, this is when you knowingly have the power and intention - directly, indirectly, or through another person - to control the whereabouts of the substance. Even if you do not have physical possession of the drug, you must be able to gain physical possession of it.

Are Drugs in My House or Car Enough to Prove Constructive Possession? It depends. Remember, close proximity to a controlled substance is never enough to prove constructive possession.

Exclusive Occupancy If you are the sole occupant of the home or car where a controlled substance is found, your exclusive occupancy is often enough to evidence your ability to exercise control over the substance and your knowledge of its presence.

Non-Exclusive Occupancy If you are not the sole occupant of the home or car, possession is slightly more difficult to prove. Where there is more than one occupant, there must be additional evidence, such as incriminating facts or circumstances, that shows both knowledge and control.

What are Incriminating Facts or Circumstances? Every jurisdiction puts a different amount of weight on specific facts or circumstances, but these are a few examples of common links between a person and a controlled substance.

- The drugs are in plain view
- The drugs are with the person's personal items
- If in a car, they are found on the same side of the car or are in the person's immediate proximity
- If in a home, they are found in the person's bedroom
- Suspicious behavior during arrest
- Ownership of smoking devices or drug paraphernalia
- Ownership or control over the place where the substance is found

Texting While Driving:
What is Texting While Driving? Texting while driving is the act of reading, viewing, writing, or sending text messages via cell phone while operating a motor vehicle. It is a moving traffic violation and in some jurisdictions it is considered to be a criminal misdemeanor. Texting while driving is highly discouraged because it distracts the driver from concentrating on road safety.

Studies have shown that texting while driving increases the risk of a vehicle crash by anywhere from 2.8 to 23.2 times than normal. Therefore, the laws covering texting are aimed more at deterrence (prevention) rather than recovery of losses.

What are the Laws on Texting While Driving? The details of state texting laws vary widely by region. For example, some only ban texting while driving for persons under the age of 18 with a temporary permit. Check with an attorney for more details regarding the texting and cell phone use laws of your particular state.

Currently 30 states and the District of Columbia have an outright ban on all forms of texting for all drivers. In 26 of these states, enforcement is primary, meaning that the police can stop a person if they see them texting while operating a motor vehicle. In the remaining four states, enforcement is secondary, meaning that a police officer can only cite the offender for texting if they have pulled them over for a different violation, such as running a stop light.

What are the Penalties for Texting While Driving? As mentioned, the laws governing texting while driving vary from state to state. However, punishment for texting while driving generally includes a combination of the following:

- **Monetary fines-** these can range from as low as $20 up to $500 depending on the state

- **Criminal charges-** in some states texting while driving can result in criminal misdemeanor charges (Class B or C)

- **Jail or prison time-** if the offense has resulted in bodily injury to another driver, jail or prison time may be imposed

The severity of punishments increases with repeat offenses. For example, after a second offense, the judge may choose to issue a higher fine or a longer jail sentence.

In addition to legal consequences, other consequences for texting while driving include:

- Points on one's driving record
- Suspension or revocation of driving privileges
- Mandatory road safety classes

- Vehicle impoundment, especially if great bodily injury resulted from an accident

Finally, in some jurisdictions commercial drivers and school bus drivers are held to stricter standards. Violations can result in fines of over $2,000 for truck and bus drivers.

For more information about the laws in your state contact an Attorney or go to www.legalmatch.com

---

So let's be clear it is up to you to keep yourself safe and to protect your own future. I wanted to add a few facts to help you consider that "Sorry", "I didn't know", or "I didn't think" will not be considered in court and you must be vigilant yourself.

Know who your friends are, who you are driving with, and talk to your parents and set up a contingency plan. Your parents know you may falter, they were teens once themselves. If you are at a party, or with friends and they are drinking **Do Not Drive Home With Them**, if you had a drink or something else **Do Not Drive Home Yourself**, call mom, call dad, even call your best friend's mom – most any of them will come and drive you home. You may have to face an argument, or a stern discussion in the morning, and own up to some consequences but they will be far less then an accident, a loss of life or the loss of your own future.

I wish you well on all these relationship challenges…J.R.

Chapter 6
REFERENCES

Selected Readings/Investments/Resources

Selected Readings

You Can Negotiate Anything
By Herb Cohen

On the best sellers list for a long time. This book is educational and witty. A must for the student who wants to have the edge in win/win negotiations with parents who are overly concerned about slowing down your teen age enthusiasm for having every possible experience before age 18, or the policeman who stops you for a speeding ticket.

Dress for Success
By John Molloy

An educational journey on what to wear to cause others to give you respect and attention. Not only will you get hired on your first interview, but also you will get the top hourly wage for your pay scale classification at that company. Every student in drama class knows how actors control their audiences by the clothes they wear. You will be in control of the job interview.

Dressing for Success

Look up in the phone book for shops in your neighborhood, or the Internet.

> **Consider:**
>
> - Suits for $12.00.
>
> - White dress shirts for $4.00.

- Designer ties or plain red or blue ties for $2.00.
- Black (not brown) dress shoes for $15.00.
- Women's look like new high fashion clothes and shoes for $5.00

Put it together as best you can and that will be good enough for the job interview even if the whole combination is slightly loose or tight.

Once you own an outfit you can rent it for a day to your friend for their job interview, and begin a clothes rental business. It might not fit, but maybe his mom can make a slight alteration. You can also use it for the school play or for your older sisters wedding.

Source For Tailor Made Clothes

Balani Custom Clothiers
55 West Monroe (Street Level)
Chicago, Illinois 60603
Ph. 1-312 263-9003

This family concern has been dressing me in suits and the rest of my family in specialty garments since 1962. They have clothing sources for materials and tailoring that are not readily available at retail. Their prices are quite satisfactory since they have all the work done overseas.

Selected Speculative Stocks

Disclaimer: None of the following are recommendations to buy any of these stocks. This is merely an academic exercise to get you involved in what is meant by a stock "symbol" or the significance of the "trading range", so when you talk to stock brokers you have some idea of what they are saying.

LEEP, Inc. (formerly known as Leading Edge Earth Products. The name was changed to LEEP at the end of 2004.)
Stock symbol LPPI
Web page www.leepinc.com
Manufacturing Plant in Williamsport, Pennsylvania USA

   This company manufacturers a new fire proof insulated panel for assembling homes. They claim it is load bearing, lightweight, hurricane, mold, termite and rodent proof. It is alleged to be earthquake resistant with an insulation factor similar to an ice chest and can be assembled for the same cost of a wooden stick built home, and at less than 40% of the time. The stock price in April 2010 was in the range of $.02 per share. Consider this stock as being as likely to go to a dollar as it is to go to a penny. I like it because it has the answer to supplying the new materials for rebuilding places like New Orleans and Mississippi after the last hurricane and all the future ones.

   The U.S. Government is currently using this product as the only approved product for the single application of a building which has a constant temperature useful for checking mail coming into the USA, which may contain mail bombs or viruses. Consider this a very, very speculative stock with a billion dollar future the same as Microsoft in 1975. My guess is that 30% of the readers of this book will be living in a LEEPCORE built home over the next 20 years.

Northern Dynasty Minerals
Stock Symbol NAK
Web site: www.pebblepartnership.com
Main office in Vancouver British Columbia, Canada.
Phone: (907) 339-2600

It is rumored, that in early 2001 they discovered the world's largest gold mine and the 2nd largest copper mine in the world. The mine is located approximately 75 miles west of Cook's Inlet across from Homer, Alaska and 16 miles from Iliamna, Alaska. The stock price in April 2010 was approximately $9.00 per share. Consider this stock as a good buy and a medium speculation

Basic Lesson on How to Choose a Stock to Buy

The Analysis Process: For Example, Products

List products you use every day:

- What Products Do You Love - Are other teens using and loving the same product?

- Pick your three favorite products.

- Research them on the internet. (Bloomburg.com is one source to find out who makes that product.

- Get their Stock symbol.

- Find the cost of a share.

- Check once a week to see how the stock is doing – your "imaginary investment".

It does not cost you anything to "paper trade" on the

computer. You and your friends can make a game and compete for some prize like a $10.00 bill to see who could take $50,000.00 of funny money that the computer program gives you to increase it beyond the other participants. Just have Dad set you up with a Stock Broker like Ameritrade, Scott Trade, Monster Trade or E-trade and put $200.00 into the account. Then leave the $200.00 alone and just use the "Paper Trading" option to have some fun and learn how the Day Trading system works.

Sources for Gold and Silver Coins or ETFs

Monex: 1-800-752-1400 – physical coins

Certified Mint: 1-800-528-1380- physical coins

Trade Monster: 1-877-598-3190 #2- ETFs

Ameritrade: 1-800-669-3900 - ETFs

If you don't want the inconvenience of having to store the actual metal in a safety deposit box, consider buying gold or silver on the American Stock Exchange under the symbol GLD or SLV. You then simply own a stock certificate backed by the actual metal. This way you get the best of both worlds. Approximate price of Gold as of April 2010 was $1100.00 per ounce. Silver at approximately $18.00 per ounce. Some people think Gold could easily go to $1600.00 over the next 4 years and Silver to $30.00. Try to understand that the paper dollars in your pocket are supported or backed up the metal itself. The backed metal is the valuable part and the paper dollars are printed just as a convenience since the metal is just too heavy to carry around. Ameritrade (1 800 669 3900) and Trade Monster (877 598 3190 Ext 2) have fixed commission in the range of $10 per trade on line.

Caddie Scholarships for College

Call the Western Golf Association
1 Briar Road, Golf, Illinois 60029
1-847-657-7556

This Scholarship is available to caddies at private golf courses and it is like living in a fraternity house at the State Universities. There is even the exception of your being able to chose a specific school if you have a special reason to go to that school. Either way you will be saving your parents over $20,000 per year in costs. They can tell you which Private Club golf courses are in your area and are offering the program.

They will pay for schools like Northwestern in Evanston, Illinois at $45,000 per year tuition, full room and some money towards other items or for a State School at approximately $20,000 per year. You have to be in the upper quarter of your class. Mom and Dad can only have a modest income and you have to caddie for approximately 150 rounds over two summers. Consider checking it out with a phone call.

Macrobiotics

Look up on Internet, Book Store or Library. One Author of prominence: ***Michio Kushi.*** This subject deals with the 1000 year old Japanese art of diagnosing human facial features to predict future health and behavior patterns of individuals.

Recognizing Emerging Billion Dollar Industries

You might want to get an entry-level job in after graduation:

Two Examples:

Stem Cells: These companies are able to take human cells from a torn or worn out section of a human body and manufacture a fluid lab culture. The fluid culture will then be injected into the wounded or worn out area and grow new cells in long chains with each chain growing more shoots just like a garden plant. This will theoretically restore the damaged or worn out area to almost its original youthful strength. Once injected into the body the fluid culture will "seek out and find its own" source at the site of the problem area. Thus, the name... Smart Cells... Imagine what this will mean to athletes, car accident victims, and lower back pain from ruptured discs, etc. When this event occurs in 6-8 years you might consider selling your stock in the pharmaceutical industries because their profits will suffer as painkillers become less popular as they once were.

Pre-implantation Genetic Diagnosis and Stem Cells: Researchers have already perfected the ability to diagnose and inform parents if a fertilized human female egg of the yet to be born child will have Down syndrome, Autism, Alzheimer's, Cancer, etc. The normal charge is approximately $1000.00.

The largest and most advanced company, to the best of my current knowledge, is called Reproductive Genetics Institute and it is located at 2825 N. Halsted Street, Chicago, Illinois 60657, Phone 773-472-4900

Bio Diesel Fuels: Companies in this industry have a new chemical to dissolve just about any vegetation or ground up trees, which then ferment the mixture to give off fumes, which then produce Ethanol. It used to be that only beans like corn or soy could be used. Imagine if we only used 30% or less of present gasoline and everything from grass clippings to jungle vegetation produced the other 70% at the same or a lower price at the gas pump.

Keep these two industries in mind when you eventually go hunting for a full time job.

Chapter 7
"BEYOND OUR BORDERS"

*"Take a chance and plant some seed.
Wait and see where it will lead."*

Teenager's In Other Countries

This section is for teenagers living in 3rd world or dictator led countries. The average American student will not be interested in what I have to say because it is just too far removed from the personal freedom that we enjoy here in the USA. Rather than not including this section in the book I thought maybe some of you in the USA would like to know that kids in some other countries are stifled or prevented from ever reaching their full potential because they are denied the "right to choose." They have to do what they are told to do, or they end up not being able to get a job. If they publicly speak up they end up in prison.

We in the USA have grown up being encouraged to experiment with everything to try to improve the world around us. The system of thinking laid out in this book works well in the United States, Canada, England, most of Europe, and some of the prominent nations on our or other continents of the world. The reason it works is because the political leaders in developed nations understand that they can make more profit off of small business net profits success, in the form of legitimate income taxes, than they could by extortion and intimidation.

Those students who live in 3rd world nations or semi-modern societies where bribery and corruption are normal, will find the local politicians doing everything they can to confiscate a good portion of their profits for themselves as they begin to succeed. If you do not pay them off, your home or office building could accidentally catch fire that night.

The politicians who demand a bribe could not care less about trying to build a student population that will build a stronger or better country to live in. They will relentlessly pressure you to give them money and justify it on the grounds that if they don't do it to you some other politician will, so they had better grab all they can get from you before other politicians get to you.

I don't have an answer as to what you should do to try to work around the tribal system in your country that has been established for over 1000 years. I can, however, encourage you, as an individual, to work within the corruption without being corrupt yourself. Consider putting your energy into becoming a leader within the corrupt political organization and put the millionaire concept on the back burner for a few years.

Once you are in position of leadership then you can gradually start to change the corrupt system from within. In that sense you will become a millionaire in that what you change will affect all your countrymen in a positive manner. As the present politicians die off you will rise to the top. You then have a choice of being equally as corrupt as your predecessor or you may begin to make your contribution to convince those in power around you that a strong middle class of independent businessmen is to be encouraged and their profits are not to be stolen from them by extortion. You can aim at the ultimate goal of directing your country to be business oriented and make it easy for individuals to get business licenses without having to payoff the clerks at the registration desk. You can encourage tribal beliefs, rituals, and privileges from ancient times to give way to a modern system of rigid rules for commerce between the buyers and sellers, along with protection for the business community from having to give up their of their profits to the local politicians as "protection money."

It may be your generation will never see the results of all your good efforts. You will however, have the satisfaction of knowing you made an attempt to change things for the better and in that sense, you are to be honored. Within all the good you try to do, you may meet stiff resistance. You may even suffer physical abuse under orders from the local dictator. However, the saving grace is that you will probably also have a standard of living above what you would have had. Consider putting out the effort to get inside the current political system to change it. I wish you well.

Notes

Chapter 8
SUMMARY

The Future

I hope you enjoyed the emotional ride through this book. Now, or twenty years from now, when you are a wealthy person, you may want to let me know what you liked or did not like in this book. I would appreciate hearing from you by e-mail:

JR@TheFutureBelongsToMe.com

Maybe, your comments would help to improve the message I want to convey to new teenagers coming up after you. It would be your contribution according to Rule #2: You can't help someone else without helping yourself. Watch immediately afterwards to see if you don't feel so good about yourself for having used your imagination to suggest something to help a new preteen coming up, that you do something right then and there to reward yourself. Maybe, you will start page one of the novel you have thought about writing for some time now, but just could not get up the nerve to put the ideas on paper.

Notes

Chapter 9
AFTERWORD

"Millionaires Guide To Becoming a Teenager"

My Next Book

I am already thinking of my next book. The title will be *"The Millionaire's Guide to Being a Teenager."* A superficial summary of the book is that most millionaires over 40 have "done it all and seen it all". Sometimes they are bored and miss the challenge of a new conquest. My first idea is to re-ignite their youthful passion and double and triple the wealth they now have by encouraging them to become part time teachers and lecturers.

University of Millionaires

My second idea is to have 200 millionaires put one million each into a pot which could be used to buy, or get donated to us, several large empty factories or warehouses in a depressed urban area and start the University of Millionaires. (In Chicago, I have identified a site just east of Cicero Avenue on Grand Avenue.) The interest from the escrow funds will pay for the overhead and the principal will not be touched without consent of 55% of the participants for expansion or other major expenses. This way, if ever the whole thing dries up, everyone gets his or her million dollars returned.

Only millionaires will be invited to teach or lecture on a rotating and as needed schedule. Each participant will be encouraged to lecture at least once a year. The pay will be $1.00 per visit and the approximate cost to the student $1.00 per lecture.

The individual experiences of each millionaire will be the unwritten textbook explaining how each has made and lost huge amounts of money. In a natural fashion, this will expand to individual counseling to young entrepreneurs. The camaraderie with fellow wealthy men and women and having a beer with the students afterwards could "spark" their purpose and change their entire attitude towards others around them as they start to loosen up.

Maybe some will feel more "complete" as they again experience the basic joy and laughter we all had in high school or college. Maybe some of you millionaires reading this will meet a new "significant other" as a personal life companion, who appreciates, rather than criticizes, how your mind is constantly focused in on financial matters, since that persons priorities are the same as yours. Also, on the lighter side, my guess is that every business minded person reading the above summary is already reaching for their cell phone to call his or her real estate broker to start looking at possibly buying cheap property in the Grand Avenue area mentioned above. A core anchor like a university could revitalize any depressed area and make a whole bunch of new millionaires in several cities in the USA. That's the legitimate way it is supposed to work and maybe you will be one of them.

If any of you millionaires reading this book would like to contribute any ideas or views, it could be good for all of us. Please reach me on the e-mail at:

JR@TheFutureBelongsToMe.com
www.TheFutureBelongsToMe.com

Chapter 10
INDIVIDUAL GOALS AFTER READING THIS BOOK

Write down your personal goals, improvements and ideas for investment in a journal.

One week: _____

_____

_____

One month: _____

_____

_____

One year: _____

_____

_____

Five years: _____

_____

_____

Suggestion for you to consider as Improvements:

Attitude - Ask yourself, "How can I be a better person?"

_____

_____

_____

Civic Responsibility - Can I donate my time/skills to a good cause?

_____

_____

_____

Appearance - List how you can improve others first impression of you so potential employers will look upon you favorably versus seeing you as "just another kid looking for a job".

_____

_____

_____

Sources for Potential Investments

Products - List products you use every day:

_____

_____

_____

What Products Do You Love? - Are other teens using and loving the same product?

_____

_____

_____

Pick 3 - Pick your three favorite products. Research on the internet - get their Stock symbol, find the cost of a share - Trade 100 shares "on paper", check once a week - what did your "investment" do? It does not cost you anything to "paper trade" on the computer and you and your friends can compete to see who would have taken $50,000.00 of funny money and increased it or lost it. Just have Dad set you up with a Stock Broker like Ameritrade, Scott Trade, Monster Trade or E-trade and put $200.00 into the account. Then leave the $200.00 alone and just use the "Paper Trading" option to have some fun and learn how the Day Trading system works.

_____

_____

_____

_____

_____

Keep a record of how you do in your Journal or on the Note Pages in this book.

Congratulations!

For Whatever It Is Worth –

If You Have Traveled To This Point Of The Book, You Have My Admiration; My Guess Is That You Will Probably Be A Winner In Whatever Occupation That You Choose.

Prelude - This is an summary to the next three Appendixes

Readers: ONENESS is the word I would like you to memorize.

According to ancient Scholars each of us has a choice. We can look in the mirror, see our body and declare that we are humans on this earth with all the everyday problems we have to face each day. The other choice is to see in the mirror a perfect physical manifestation of every invisible idea that could possibly exist. Perfect mechanical engineering, perfect fluid dynamics, perfect balance, dexterity, vision, hearing, outer skin for protection, etc.

In a Metaphysical sense your individual physical manifestation (body) is merely Divine Consciousness manifesting IT'S self "as" HIS Personality here on Earth through your body so HE can function on a material plane. You have to consider accepting the argument that all we humans exist only for HIM to have a physical medium to work through. Remember, HE is 100% invisible and takes up all space. This is called being Omni-present. You and I can't see anything invisible, so for HIS own reasons he needs that body of yours to get his work or purposes done here on Earth.

Most every Religion here on Earth teaches that HE is "up there" and you are "down here" and if you perform a huge volume of repetitive rituals HE might throw you a bone now and then. It is up to you to find a quiet place to meditate on what I have said in the above paragraphs. The goal of this is for you to see with HIS eyes, hear with HIS ears and have a marvelous human experience every day of your life. I wish you well.

If any of you are skeptical on what I have said above, consider reading: Luke 17:21, Psalm 16.5, John 6.45, Prov 1.7 and Matt 6.6.

Notes

APPENDIX I
Brief Explanation of Metaphysics

The reason this subject has been put at the end of this book is because it may not be meaningful to most of you. At age 17 your brain is just too soggy to handle the challenge. It is the same reason High School courses are not taught in Grammar School. However, it is significantly meaningful to me. I want to share it with you because this subject has been the foundation of my financial success. On everyday activities, you might even stretch the "meaningful" aspect by saying it guided me from being a run-of-the-mill-50-year-old, who was not going anywhere, to a 64 year old in the year 2000 who finished 10th in the nation, representing Illinois, in the Senior Olympics 400 meter with a time of 1:136 as well as winning gold and silver medals in the 200 meter in Illinois competitions. It also guided me to "discover" how to earn what modest wealth I have accumulated over the past 20 years.

This subject is a marvelous challenge for teenagers who are looking, with pen in hand (now a computer), to write a best seller with their first book. Consider this subject as "boot camp" - a place to start since it will demand not only excellence in journalism, but research on readily available materials that will spin your head in several different directions.

By the time you spend a year studying this subject, you will be torn between the two diametrically opposed camps and it will push to you to a state of humility. After this, any other subject you choose to write on will be a relief compared to Metaphysics.

IDEAS vs. BELIEFS, essentially is the subject of

Metaphysics. You can gain a position of prominence within your group if you understand these two diametrically opposed concepts since every adult, in their own way, is searching for the Truth about why they exist in the first place.

Consider using the library or the Internet to look up the definitions of Reality and Unreality. You will find that things that are REAL never change and things that constantly change are Unreal. Notice that everything in the material world is constantly shrinking or expanding so it falls into the definition of being Unreal. Logically then... "If you can see it, feel it or taste it, then it is Not Real".

Imagine the reaction of your friends when you declare that a car or your own body is not real. They will not want to hear that all the material objects you can see are just illusions or reflections of Ideas. If it is invisible, as Ideas are, then it is Real. You have to keep these observations to yourself or your friends will think you are strange, even though you are declaring the Truth.

You will have to decide which of two opposites you think is the way to go.

One will be that your body is just a costume that you wear for approximately 6 to 60 years and when it wears out (you die) nothing changes. Your consciousness merely gets a new costume in the form of a newborn baby somewhere in the Universe (i.e. matter passes through life).

The Second will be the popular religious teachings that when your body dies, you die. (i.e. life is in matter).

Next time you are out on a date with a group and the

conversation starts to drag, consider bringing up this subject and feeding the group with a few of the basics mentioned previously as best you can. Then settle back and watch the fireworks. It can be fun and no one can prove that anyone is correct or incorrect.

Notes

Appendix II
Healing Yourself: This is a deeper analysis of Appendix I

Let's address the core issue of all mental healing, as follows: According to the ancient writers the key to healing yourself mentally is to realize that the well known teaching by religious leaders that "you are made in the image and likeness of..." or "I and my Father are one", or "of myself I do nothing, but through me Divine Consciousness does everything" <u>*refers to your invisible consciousness and not your body.*</u> Divine Consciousness is invisible. HE has no shape or form. He takes up all space. Therefore, you, as HIS image and likeness have to be invisible and not material. If you accept this then the previous statements all make sense. Try to see your body as a costume that you drag around with you until you lose it by chance or by choice. Try to see that when you lose your current body nothing changes. According to these ancient writers when you die, you don't go anywhere. The reason you don't go anywhere is that you are "there" already. "There" is another name for Heaven. Later on in this chapter you will read how these ancient writers attempt to prove there is no Hell or Devil.

If your first reaction to the concept of healing yourself by the quality of your thought is one of rejection because you are so accustomed to getting healed from illness by a shot, a pill or some herb, then apply this logic to test the theory. Try to "blush" right now without any embarrassment to assist you. Can't be done. At some time in the future, try not to "blush" when you really are embarrassed. Can't be done. What this proves is that your thought controls your body and in the case of self-condemnation generally makes you sick. If you feel good about yourself your thoughts are joyous, which keeps a smile on your face. The result then is you're a happy person and feeling good.

Just watch when you are really angry with yourself for having made a mistake. Suddenly find that you have a physical pain in some part of your body. The pain will range from a headache to facial damage from speeding and ramming into the car in front of you. Your body or costume merely reflects what is going on in that head of yours. That is why I went into detail in the first few chapters of this book so as to encourage you to see yourself as a good person. In business it is the "two rules" that support a good image of yourself. How can you score on the soccer or other playing field if you are all distracted in your thought because things are not working out with Mom and Dad or your girl or boyfriend?

Albert Einstein, one of the greatest thinkers of our time was heavily into this subject. One of his theories that agrees with many other writers on the subject is that the past and the future are not real. The only Realty is this particular moment of your life… *so enjoy it and quit worrying so much about what happened yesterday or what might happen tomorrow.* In many ways I think the subject should be in a book by itself. However, you may never get around to reading another book on the subject so why not try to store a few of the ideas I have mentioned in your memory.

Allow yourself to be aware that most all your successes in the business world and in your personal life here on Earth result from rewarding yourself. *Healing yourself* of health problems, financial losses, loss of companionship, a loved one, or whatever else ails you is *the promised reward for studying Metaphysics.*

As you get into understanding the Realty of the invisible Ideas right in front of you and the Unreality of the material object you are staring at right this moment, you will find that each day that you continually end up in just the right spot at just the right time on an on going basis. This also, is the promised reward of studying Metaphysics.

As you read what I have written, you will find that I am explaining the simple concept of self-healing from many different angles. At your young age, it is too much to expect you to grasp what I am saying in one reading. You may interpret some paragraphs as repetitive. Just bear with it. I am giving you my best shot at explaining in several thousand words, that which could be summarized in one sentence... "That which is REAL (Ideas) and that which is an ILLUSION of REALTY (Matter - same as Beliefs)". This is heavy stuff, and if you are tempted to close the book, go ahead. On the other hand, if you are up to the challenge the same as putting just a few more pounds on the weight bar just to see if you can still make the Press... girls... you can create your own example. You can then expect to have a feeling of discovery and elation that is priceless.

As you read, try to have a few laughs along with a feeling of warmth and being protected by the BOSS HIMSELF.

The concept that supports all these good things coming your way is really quite simple and clear. *All the GOOD things we all want are in place already and our job is to discover them.* The reason the "cure" does not happen immediately is because people have so many established view points, habits and personal preferences to wash out of their though. Until that is accomplished they can't see what is right in front of them. All of us want to hang on to the familiar, and this blocks out our discovering the answer to our immediate problem.

Pause and write down any questions that come to mind in your Journal.

None of the Good (Ideas) we want or need to lead us out of our frustration or aggravation is created just for us. They are in place right this minute and will always be available to every human being who is willing to pay the price of letting go of all the selfish Beliefs he or she holds near and dear at this moment. Most adults would rather go to the grave with all the pain and suffering attached to their beliefs on religion, politics, sex, money, etc. rather than washing all the old out and discovering the new.

You have, as a teenager, the advantage of being innocent, and uncomplicated and spontaneous. You have very little scar tissue from ugly experiences. If you, as a teenager, studied Metaphysics at this early age there is good chance you would develop a frame of mind that is modestly detached from Matter. *You would understand that it is only your interpretation of human events in your thought that makes you happy or sad.* The event itself of being elected Captain of the Soccer or Hockey Team or being named Prom Queen is just another human experience. Of themselves, neither of these most pleasant awards has any more value than you personally give to them.

To heal yourself of some current dilemma that has you temporarily bent out of shape try this experiment. Just close your eyes and see yourself as invisible. See yourself as a pure, invisible, radiant, and joyous Consciousness. With your eyes still closed, visualize all the material things around you, including your body, as dumb matter without any life or intelligence. Hold that image in your thought for a count of 5. Then open your eyes and go about your normal activity. When it is convenient, repeat the experiment. Each time, try to hold the image of your invisible "Essence" or Consciousness in your thought, for a few more seconds. Realizing that I am repeating myself for clarification purposes ... "your Consciousness is that invisible part of you which is rational and perceptive and which makes you different from the animals of the forest. ***Your Consciousness is that part of you that laughs and cries and allows you to read and write... animals can't do that."*** Animals only have a mortal mind, which is concerned with food, sex and survival. When they die all the carbon that their body is made of dissolves into the soil and that is the end of that individual animal. You also, have an animal body that will dissolve back into the soil, but your invisible Consciousness will live forever. Your Consciousness is the part of you that is reading this book right now. It can never die because it never was born.

You never had a beginning. You just "were". You are now and have always been.

The logic to support this observation is that your Consciousness is derived from DIVINE CONSCIOUS- NESS who takes up all space. You are part of HIS Expression of HIMSELF, and in that sense, you are Immortal. Each of us on this earth is equal and identical as regards our Consciousness or "Being". Each of us always "was", is now and always will "be". That part of us can never die because we are Divine Consciousness' expression of ITSELF. HE had no beginning. HE just "was" and will always "be".

Let's assume you are saying to yourself ... "so what

value is all this analysis?" The value of this awareness is that you may begin to see your body as a non-intelligent costume. You may start seeing all material objects as dumb matter that you have control over. *You may start to see that you can control your body with your thought rather than your body controlling you regarding* sickness or strength of purpose.

When you can appreciate the magnificence of your own Consciousness you start to feel part of something powerful. In the original Star Wars movie, what I have just said was referred to as *"May the force go with you."*

How many of you grasped the message from the movie The Matrix? The message was that our bodies imprison our Consciousness. When we break free from the confines of our body we are then able to free others who are trapped by their bodies and everyone lives happily ever after.

The author of the *Da Vinci Code,* Dan Brown has a new book called The Lost Symbol. It is an exciting and entertaining account of good guys and bad guys and well worth your time to read it. I mention it since he confirms that scholars and healers have advocated what I am saying to you for centuries. I like the part where his scientist heroine declares that the human body loses a tiny fraction of weight when the body stops living. That weight is then judged as your Soul or your Consciousness, which is leaving the body since it lives forever, and your body is merely a costume or carbon form that has no more value than you give it. He proves up how scholars of the past have demonstrated that your *individual Consciousness has sufficient power to heal your own body of contamination such as cancer or damaged body parts.*

He then explains how your Consciousness, when grouped with other's Consciousness, could then be used as a weapon to make major changes in the world's Belief system regarding such things as religious hatred, or bringing rain to drought areas or diverting the path of a hurricane, etc. This is the machine that the heroine is working on in the lab and what the bad guy wants to destroy since it means that everyone could be "All Powerful". The bad guy wants the scientific formula from the machine for himself so he can be the only one who is "All Powerful". He then wants to rule the Earth. By destroying the formula after he is "All Powerful", he eliminates any competition. If you just want to pick out a few of these examples, I have noted the pages in his book for you to glance at, as follows: 58- 59- 76- 314- 318- 454- 467- 468- 492- 495- 499- 500- 501 and 502.

Getting back to each of you finding a way to heal your own problems, my suggestion is that you continue to think about this exercise of closing your eyes, to visualize your own invisible Consciousness, and you will find yourself getting more and more relaxed. You will now have a tool to work with for neutralizing any dilemma that has you temporarily off balance.

Pause and write down any questions that come to mind in your Journal or on the following Note pages

Breakthroughs

Nowadays, running a 4-minute mile is commonplace among athletes. Before it actually happened, everyone in both the scientific and the athletic departments said it could not humanly be done. Then one person refused to accept that Belief and ran the race in less than 4 minutes. My memory says his name was Roger Bannister, but I could be mistaken. Soon after that Belief was shattered, more and more runners were able to accomplish the same result. Consider going on the Internet to read story after story of individuals who have accomplish fantastic breakthroughs (Stem cell research is an example) which everyone said could not be done. Once a single individual destroyed the Belief, lots of people found they could do the same thing. It was the universal belief that held it back for such a long period of time. *Eliminate the Belief and you eliminate the problem.*

These are examples of why you might consider studying Metaphysics for good health along with becoming a Millionaire before you are 35 years old.

The answer to dissolving every obstacle you may encounter in the future is available to all of you who are reading this Chapter. The price you pay for this giant reward of having command of the material world around you is a steady effort on your part to break free in your thought, from the common Belief that there is Life, or Intelligence **inside** your body. The authors who advocate "Breaking Free," insist that Life, and Intelligence take up all space and your body merely passes through them during the short period of your human experience. They see your body as just a temporary costume and declare that your body is merely an inert carbon form without any special value. The only real part of you is your unchangeable invisible Consciousness.

To repeat… **your body is just a "costume",** and some writers conclude that soon as you lose your old costume, you merely get a new one in the form of newly born baby somewhere in our Universe. Maybe you can immediately see the value of this Understanding because it dissolves fear of death. Once fear is dissolved there is no limit to what you can accomplish during your human experience. Imagine how many older people would suddenly relax and enjoy or tolerate their last years on this earth because they could look forward to their next human experience with the excitement of a new "boy-girl" thing and a healthy new body.

Take me as an example. For 40 years I have enjoyed entertaining at family gatherings with rhymes and poems about what was going on with the entire family. At the same time I had the "belief" that you had to graduate from journalism school with a superior command of the English language in order to write a book. Right now you are reading "that" book. I did not go through any formal journalism teaching. I suspect my lack of technical formal training is evident to some of you, but I am writing from my heart and not my head.

This is exactly what makes writing this book so enjoyable. I know that even before I start typing, the words will flow out onto the page. I am merely the messenger boy for the delivery of the concepts or ideas that you will hopefully use to have a more rewarding and semi-problem free human experience. It is not that you won't have all the problems that each of us has during our lifetime. It is that you will see them as "just another problem". You will be upset and fuss around for a short period of time, but you will then get a hold of yourself and calm down.

Think about how comforting and reassuring it will be to know that Divine Consciousness already knows all the facts about your distress. ***Focus on HIS presence being all around you,*** and soon as you ask HIM to evaporate the Beliefs that are emotionally strangling you; HE will go to work on your behalf. You still have to do all the human stuff to make it all come together, but *HE clears the way for you to either escape or progress.* See HIM as your teammate or Coach. If you can allow yourself to practice the experiment of closing your eyes for 5 or 10 seconds, and focus on seeing your individual Consciousness being ONE with DIVINE CONSCIOUSNESS, the results you are looking for should show up in rapid fashion.

From my experience the results show up SILENTLY.

The results won't even be noticeable until you look back a week or some time later and suddenly realize that what was bothering you has evaporated. When this "looking back" event starts to occur over and over again you will find that people will start to comment..." How does John or Jane always seem to have a handle on just what to do as problems come up?"

Take my case from my high school experience. My educational background was a public high school called Amundsen on the north side of Chicago. I had 16 athletic letters on my Letterman Sweater but graduated in the upper quarter of my class without knowing the difference between a THEME and a THESIS. I almost failed English 1A at the University of Wisconsin at the end of the first semester. The teacher felt sorry for me and gave me a D. He saw I was trying really hard to make up in one semester that which I should have been taught over four years in High School. I went to College without knowing how to read or write the English language effectively.

I was convinced that there was a way to learn how to

read and write so and I set out to discover what was right in front of me, but at first, I just could not clearly see it... I still remember how painful it was (to the point of getting headaches) to climb such a steep educational hill in such a short time. However, each challenge of the learning process melted right in front of me as I destroyed every human belief that was telling me I could not succeed in doing in 12 weeks that which I should have been taught in 4 years of High School.

Those of you, who are in Public High School, with the exception of a few experimental public schools or those, which are in expensive neighborhoods, are going to be super frustrated during your first year in College. This is because of the current less than perfect emphasis on studying the English language. Unless you learn to read and write English effectively you will end up at the bottom of the food chain, when you fail at the end of your first year and go to work in some factory for an hourly wage.

In my case I eventually went on to law school, passed the BAR and still occasionally practice Law in Illinois. I mainly step up in front of the Judge when one of the kids or grandchildren wants to avoid a large fine in Traffic Court at zero expense to them... I suspect you, as a teenager, can relate to that!

The point here is that you too can get rid of Beliefs that are holding you back. You can't do it with your own will power alone. You have to understand that it is your realization that right this moment you have access to all the knowledge of the Universe. That realization is the magic that makes you suddenly special to yourself. Why? Because your Consciousness comes from and is directly connected to DIVINE CONSCIOUSNESS. In the business world here on Earth we call it "insider's information".

DIVINE CONSCIOUSNESS will give you an Idea to guide you to move to the right or the left or to stand or run. Remember HE is not "up there" on a cloud somewhere. HE is all around you and because you and HE are one, HE will protect you if you just take the time to ask HIM. His everyday job is to evaporate ugly human beliefs when called upon. By seeing the bad guy as being "one Consciousness" with DIVINE CONSCIOUSNESS the same as you yourself, you are automatically calling on HIM to neutralize the aggravating Beliefs of the bad guy.

This method is a great way to have a smile on your face all day long because you now know that you have the ultimate weapon to attempt to neutralize any challenge facing you.

Pause and write down any questions that come to mind in your Journal or on the following Note pages.

If you see all this self-healing as a lot of words and would rather rely on human weapons to fight back with, then, you are in for uncertainty and sleepless nights. Look at the kids around you with the fingernails that are all but chewed off or cuticles that are picked to where they are bleeding. These kids are trying to solve their problems by themselves. It can't be done. They will crash and burn trying to escape the fear and uncertainty in their head. If you currently hang with anyone who is bent out of shape over some event in their life, consider reaching out to them with some words of encouragement based on what I am trying to teach you in this chapter. At minimum, you will feel good about yourself, and reward yourself for the effort you put out to help someone else. Everyone wins when you unselfishly extend yourself.

Consider giving this method a chance to prove itself. It really is the ultimate weapon for defense. Results, which come from this understanding, are that you start to notice that everything else in your human experience starts to connect in a favorable manner. Problems at home start to lose their cutting edge. The girl or boy at school who you are interested in suddenly notices you. Your close friends start saying things like..." what is going on? You seem so different!"

Divine Consciousness is always available for you to talk with. He knows everything. You don't even have to explain your problem or emergency to HIM. HE knows all the facts already, because he knows everything that ever was, is now or ever will be. *To HIM all of existence is single moment,* just like Albert Einstein's wrote about.

Try to imagine what it would be like to know everything that happened in the past and everything that will happen in the future. There would be no need to keep a scrapbook or any need to anticipate what you and your friends will be doing this weekend. You would be aware of everything all at once. There would be nothing for you to fear because everything would be "certain". If you continue thinking about this and repeating the experiment you will find yourself becoming more and more relaxed about whatever dilemma has you off balance.

If you hang onto this experience and repeat it every time you are mentally bent out of shape, you will find that you will gradually start to see a solution to every problem.

The solution has been in place since time began, just waiting for you to discover it.

Whether you are the quarterback of the football team and it 4th down on the 1 yard line with only 3 seconds left on the clock, or in the Miss America Pageant, and you have to intelligently answer the Judge's question, you will see how the event, at that moment is no different from any other event. You will see the football play as "just another play like any other play" or for the girls "just another question like any other question". You could never do this if you placed any real value on either situation. Your fear of failure on the sports field or the embarrassment of not answering the Judge's question properly would take control of you and your mind would be frozen.

You want to win in each case, so you give it your best shot, but if you see that dealing with this challenge is just another human event, like all other human events, then just the perfect play or the perfect answer to the Judges will suddenly be right in front of you. In both examples is will be like reading the invisible answer off of an invisible piece of paper right in front of you. When you win the contest, it will be a pleasant experience, and you will be all smiles, but you will take it all in stride as a normal happening that you earned. It is not a "big deal" one way or another. The joy is in knowing that you "let it all out" and gave it your best shot. The scorecard will take care of itself.

To repeat, I am merely the messenger boy for the delivery to you, via this book of concepts or ideas so that you will have a more rewarding and problem free human experience. Remember, humans don't create anything...

they merely discover what was there all along. My book is merely the instrument for delivering to your doorstep the words and ideas in a form that a teenager can understand. Hopefully, this book will make a big difference in your future financial human experience. Also, you may notice that if you can discipline yourself to practice this experiment the results will show up almost immediately. Everything that is best for you will happen in SILENCE.

The following is a summary of the past few pages. Go over it slowly and try to mentally feel the significance of each statement.

All Good is in place already in the form of Ideas.

Your job is to see Ideas as the only REALTY since they never change.

Your job is to see that matter is just an illusion of REALTY and without any substance since matter is constantly expanding or contracting. (These are very difficult concepts to swallow until you experiment with the closed eye routine and find out a short time later your problem has evaporated.)

If you ever get to the point of "Understanding" then every day of your human life will have a lightness and joy attached to it. You will find that when others are all bent out of shape and fearful, you will be like your favorite movie hero who is calm and collective in a dangerous situation. Your understanding that there is a way out of the threatening situation, and that all you have to do is ask the BOSS for a sense of direction to discover it, will put you in command.

Now... what supports the contention that all Good is

already in place? Most people believe that "Good" and "Evil" are like warriors that co-exist in some constant struggle for superiority. Keep in mind that this is what I have learned from reading the writings of others and not any original thoughts of my own. Try to hold a steady focus as I explain in clumsy human language how it allegedly works, as follows:

1. There is only one invisible DIVINE CONSCIOUSNESS

2. DIVINE CONSCIOUSNESS is 100% GOOD.

3. HE (abbreviated for typing convenience) takes up all space.

4. HE is called by a different name by each tribe of people on this planet (Allah, Buddha, God, Jehovah, Mohammad, etc.)

5. If HE takes up all space, there is no room for HIS, HER or ITS opposite.

6. Therefore, only invisible GOOD has substance and exists as an unchanging Realty.

7. If only Good (Heaven) exists then anything called Bad (Hell or the Devil or Evil) can't exist.

8. Human teachers try to scare little children into believing that the Devil and Hell really exist so when the scared little children grow up into scared adults they put more money on the collection plate to buy their way into Heaven.

9. Heaven is not a place. Heaven is a concept or idea.

10. Heaven takes up all space and is all around you right

at this moment. It is just another name for Divine Consciousness who takes up all space... they are one and the same.

So much for my amateur manner of summarizing about how only GOOD exists as a REALITY.

Moral of the story: Just relax and enjoy every minute of everyday. Divine Consciousness will provide you with a sense of direction if you yield to HIS guidance as the Ultimate Weapon to confront any problem.

Why don't you take a pause now and go freshen up and have something to drink before continuing.

Pause and write down any questions / observations in your Journal or Note pages that come to mind.

Now that you have recharged, let's move onto another view or proof for Divine Consciousness's oneness with each of you. For convenience sake, let's call Divine Consciousness HIM rather than HE, SHE or IT. Bear with my need to repeat some of the words used in previous paragraphs. Try to see that you have a Consciousness that allows you to laugh, cry, be articulate, and perceptive. Try to see your body as nothing more than a carbon form same as any animal running around the forest. For our purposes here, we will refer to your current body as your current "costume" same as any other animal. You wear your current costume for 8 seconds or 80 years and when it wears out by choice or by chance, it returns to the soil it came from just like any other animal on the planet.

Writers guess, and it is only a logical conclusion without any proof to back it up, that all that happens after you lose your present human costume is that you instantly or eventually get another one in the form of a new baby just born somewhere in the Universe. This they argue is **the natural and necessary Balancing of the Universe.**

WHAT DOES "BALANCE OF THE UNIVERSE" HAVE TO DO WITH METAPHYSICS?

The answer to that question is that Balance is an Idea. It comes from Divine Consciousness HIMSELF. The material symbols or events such as catching a football, dying or being born, winning a soccer game, earthquakes, air plane crashes, of floods, occurring, bombs exploding in Iraq etc. are all necessary at just that moment to form a "whole". One event balances the other.

Divine Consciousness is concerned with the balancing the overall picture of the entire Universe. You and I have to be concerned with not being in just the wrong place at the wrong time here on Earth. The way we avoid that aggravation is to have a human body that is free of energy blocks that need to be released by a painful massage. Within both Metaphysical and human theory, if your body is free of drugs, alcohol, cigarette tar or other contamination, you do not experience any energy blocks, so you have a relatively carefree human experience. If your body is free of physical or chemical contamination there is no need for a painful "massage" to break or remove your energy blocks. For example, it would be a similar analysis as to why people go to Chiropractors to get their backs "popped". The overall claim is that once the energy block is removed, the energy of Universe flows more freely through your body and you feel good again. If you are an athlete you know how well you perform when you body feels free of restrictions. Notice how some people "pop" their fingers or their neck themselves. They are removing the minor discomfort and restoring themselves to balance.

What if they did not "pop" their finger and ignored the uncomfortable feeling? The probability is that they would catch that finger on something and with a great deal of pain that finger would get "popped". If the jam in the finger was not addressed it might be that other symptoms would arise and it would take a tragic car accident in order to massage your entire body so as to restore balance to the Universe. Moral of the story... don't challenge the FORCE itself... you will lose every time. Other writers dramatize the concept by alleging theoretically, that if a single grain of sand or a shooting star was not where it was supposed to be every instant, the entire Universe would spin out of control. Everything might crash into everything else and only a Universal dust cloud would exist. Gradually, over billions of years the dust particles would probably gather into small balls of dirt. Gradually, the balls of dirt would become new planets, and life as we appreciate it, would start over again.

These writers who advocate the predisposed need of the Universe to constantly be in BALANCE, rationalize that everything that happens to you, me, any animal, or any change in the earth's surface (heat, cold, drought earthquakes, etc.), is necessary I don't like accepting the idea that if something happens to me or one of my family I have to write it off as "necessary", but my logic draws me to that uncomfortable conclusion.

For example, there are writers who suggest that gradually the microorganisms in the dirt of this newly formed planet would become fish or reptiles and gradually would become sophisticated animals as we see in the jungle today. Then continuing within this scenario, space travelers from another dimension might show up on some exploratory venture. They could find a planet like Earth with lots of natural beauty, and an atmosphere of oxygen that they, as space travelers could not survive in. They would see all the animals of that time running around doing little more than eating or being eaten. Let's assume that these space travelers can't live on this planet called Earth. Maybe some guy by the name of Eden, who was the space ships physician, would volunteer to start up an experimental farm on this planet called Earth to see if he could take cells from his or anybody on the space ship, and after creating a medical culture or serum (like Stem Cell research is current exploring) he would perform some experiments on these animals. His motive could be to give the planet Earth some more purpose than just a zoo. Maybe he has done this on other Planets with other creatures in an attempt to make the Universe a better place to live. Regardless of his motive, after he formulates a liquid culture, let's say he captures a goat from what is now known as France, a sheep from what is now known as Israel, a black, yellow or red monkey from what is now called Africa, China or Asia, a brown bear from Russia or a black bear from what is called Germany today. He gives these animals a steady series of injections. He would be injecting space traveler's Consciousness into Earth's animals so they could start to think and talk.

Ancient Greek writers who advocate this theory justify their views by examples. They claim that failed laboratory experiments on animals are what produced the mythological stories about King Neptune (half man and half whale), Pan (half man and half horse), and Mermaids (half female and half fish). Because these laboratory mistakes no longer served their purpose, they were released from Eden's Research Farm back into wild and observed by other humans to create the fables of today. With successful experiments, over a period of time, those animals then became intelligent "human like" animals. The animals begin to shed their body hair or protective skin and start to gradually walk uprightly. Then over millions of years they develop an advance human society similar to or superior to what we have today.

Then the cycle of growth and destruction starts over again as the selfish Beliefs of men cause atomic wars and kill off all but a few survivors. The dust in the sky blocks out the sunlight and for a million years Earth experiences another Ice Age. Take a look at a world map or globe on someone desk. Notice how Africa, if it were shifted onto the Eastern edge of Central America, would be a perfect physical fit. This leads to the belief that at one time all of Europe and Africa were part of North, Central and South America. Some tremendous explosion 100 million years ago caused the fracture that separated the two continents. It could have been a natural disaster or maybe an atomic war. The remaining human survivors were forced to revert back to primitive ways, which today would be called the caveman era. Possibly, the atomic radiation distorted the physical appearance of the previous superior humans so they degenerated to the likeness of what you see in the Natural History Museums. However, the one thing that was not destroyed or altered in any way was human CONSCIOUSNESS, because it is invisible and comes from a source that is unaffected by any human events.

Many of these writers are trying to logically explain the past to you, so you as readers, can better adapt to the future. **Think of all the money you can make by understanding the need for Balance.** You will be able to view current world or neighborhood events and anticipate what you think could happen in the immediate future. This could neutralize or balance what you think maybe getting out of balance based on everyday greed from businessmen and Politicians. Example: Picture yourself buying Gold at $1100.00 per ounce today. You see it has gone up in value from $900.00 two months ago to $1100.00 and you think it will go higher. Two months later the price is $1300.00 per ounce because it is likely that the value of the dollar has been diluted in the process from printing billions and billions of paper dollars without any having Gold in the U.S. Mint to back it up. You then anticipate that it will probably go to $1600.00 and then fall back to a lower price near $1400.00. You have Dad put in a price with the Broker to sell at $1600.00. The reason you do this is because you anticipate the natural "balance" of the Universe wherein everything that goes too high or too low will naturally drift back to some center position. It is called "catching the next wave" the same as if you were surfboarding.

PEOPLE WHO WRITE ABOUT METAPHYSICS UPSET A LOT OF READERS.

Now, most adults just do not want to hear these writer's opinions because they seem so foreign. The adults would have to give up their current Beliefs, to in order to accept the following logical, but unfamiliar opinions as follows:

"When you lose your present human costume, nothing changes. You don't go anywhere. The reason you do not go anywhere is because there is no place to go. Hell does not exist and your Consciousness has been a part of

Heaven since the beginning of time. Your Consciousness comes from Divine Consciousness. *__Have you ever heard "I and my Father are one"? That refers to the invisible part of you and not your body.__*

When you finish reading this page... YOU MUST NOW CHOOSE... one or the other... there is no middle ground.

Bottom line of what these authors say:

Your Consciousness is the only valuable part of you. In that sense you live forever the same as DIVINE CONSCIOUSNESS.

In that sense you take up a part of all space the same way a drop of water takes up part of the ocean. The drop of water exists and comes from the ocean while at the same time the ocean exists because it is made up of the drops of water. Each can only exist as part of the other.

These writers try to justify their contention that Heaven exists all around you and Hell never did exist. This is justified by the following:

Most everyone will agree that Heaven is a good place by definition and Hell is a BAD place. GOOD in their opinion is a synonym for IDEAS. Ideas are 100% good, and if you gather them all together you end up with Heaven. Ideas are Realty (confirm Reality in the Dictionary) since they never change nor does Divine Consciousness or Heaven ever change.

Human beliefs are unreal since they constantly change (confirm unreality in the dictionary). They have no roots. Whatever policy declaration some political or religious leader, or even the leader of your own teen age group, declares as law this year most likely will be changed next year. A year later the new group leaders will change those rules to fit their own selfish or charitable needs. The writers, which I continually refer to, are not against any specific leaders of politics or religious groups. These writers just don't like other humans forcing their beliefs on them.

You probably have never heard of the Masons. It is an organization that does charitable work. Many of their members are among the elite and wealthy of our society here in the USA. The group came into existence in approximately 1400 A.D. as a secret society of men who could read, write and build the large palaces and homes for the Kings and other rulers of that period. They were stonemasons who built the large buildings we see today, thus the name Masons or Masonic Order. They had the highest degree of technical training during the Dark Ages and were persecuted by religious groups because they were educated.

To me all rivers lead to the same ocean so I respect all religious and political views as being equal. You might consider this viewpoint as a worthwhile starting point in dealing with this subject. I am told the Masons accept members based on high character achievement with no discrimination because of race, religion or pedigree, but you would have to look into all the details yourself if their viewpoint appeals to you. The book the Da Vinci Code is based on such historical fact. Today the Mason organization raises money with activities such as the Shriner Circus or by passing out candy bars at auto intersections, and asking for donations to support their charitable work... especially for children's medical needs. George Washington and Thomas Jefferson are alleged to have been Masons. They wrote the Constitution to give religious and political freedom to everyone on the grounds that **everyone is entitled to their own beliefs** so long as no one tries to force those Beliefs on the other guy. Look at the back of your dollar bill and observe all the symbols that come from the Mason's influence on our American heritage and freedom to express oneself.

Since some writers say that Metaphysics proves that hell does not exist they frequently encourage readers to test their position on this issue. They start out by saying... "Let's say that hell does exist. If you are doing bad things here on earth your invisible soul will go there after your body dies and you will be tortured for all eternity." Then they pose the question: "if your soul is *invisible*, and it travels *upward* after death to enjoy drinking wine and all the other pleasures of the body, or travels *downwards* to drink vinegar for all eternity, how could it then enjoy one or suffer under the other if your soul is invisible." They argue as follows:

"We all agree that the body is left behind here on earth, so the only thing the alleged Devil can torture is something invisible. What is he going to torture? They say the worst punishment would be a scowl or he would stick his tongue out at you. You are invisible and the Devil would have to be invisible in order to even see or have contact with you."

One writer uses the following as an example:

Remember the movie The Wizard of Oz? Remember how the 20 foot tall Wicked Witch of the North had the little girl Dorothy, the Tin Man, the Lion and the Straw man convinced she, the witch, was REAL. It was all an ILLUSION of her power that could hurt the four of them.

They were all convinced the Witch was all-powerful (Beliefs) and the four of them were helpless to resist. Soon as the 12-year old girl got up the courage to pour cold water (Ideas) on the Witch, the witch screamed and screamed as she shrunk to the size of a grain of sand and then evaporated. It was all an illusion of Reality. All that was left was the little old man with a microphone who had been hiding under the wicked witch's skirt. He just wanted to create an ILLUSION OF REALTY (politicians, religious Leaders, or your own teenage Bullies) so he or she could be important, instead of just a little old man with nothing much to do all day.

The attempted proofs by these other writers about the non-existent Devil, and Hell, along with and omnipresence of Heaven will have some adults in a rage. Such individuals will construe my summary of what other authors of Metaphysics have written as a bad thing for teenagers to read. A few years ago reading Marx on his Communist ideas was sufficient to get you fired from your job. Now some high schools have it as required reading in Political Science classes. I am gambling that anyone reading my book will see it as my attempt to convey information in summary form, about many of the books in the Library that advocate the same view point as I have just referenced. Everything you have read has already been written by authors dating back to the early Greeks and is sitting on the bookshelves of your local Library and probably on the Internet as well. Someday when you become an adult you will appreciate what a great nation of laws we Americans live under. Freedom of speech and expression is what allows us to progress.

My game plan is not to upset anyone, but to point out to

teenagers what tools are available to them when they have a problem. My summary, of the scientific analysis by other writers, is my attempt to provide a single method of handling every problem a teenager could possibly have. There are so many books on the subject I am unable to suggest any one or two. Just take a chance and pick one by the cover, like most people do, when they buy a book, and run with it until you see it is just a lot of words that do not lead anywhere. If you can't satisfy yourself then consider re-reading what I have written. That should be sufficient to meet most of your needs.

Some of you teenagers are going to have an extreme problem with the Metaphysical view that declares the Devil does not exist. This will be especially true if your teachers are those who you trust and respect. You might argue that there must be a Devil or else... where would all the suffering in the world come from? The answer to that question has already been addressed in the previous paragraphs on BALANCE OF THE UNIVERSE... the ugly material event was necessary. Another teenager reading this, who will really come right off the wall with anger, is the one that has been self brainwashed. He or she is so convinced they are going to Hell for whatever they did in the past to hurt other people that they want to prove their loyalty to the Devil. They want to get on the "good side" of the Devil by honoring the Devil with every vicious thing they can do to hurt others while alive here on earth. Maybe the Devil will go easy on them in the torture chamber when they get to Hell. This is usually the motivation behind Serial killers

To repeat, this is really heavy stuff for any teenager to digest, so if you don't get it, don't worry about it. When you are really hurting inside because of some immediate trauma, you might consider trying to attain more Wisdom and Understanding by using the tools I have laid out for you. It is alleged to be a painless cure for all that ails you and once you see results, you will probably never go back to thinking that there is Life or Intelligence in matter.

As we end our superficial analysis of Metaphysics consider memorizing the following so you will have something tangible to think about and to guide you if you decide to write or study the subject, as follows:

1. DIVINE CONSCIOUSNESS is the only substance or Ego in all of existence.

2. DIVINE CONSCIOUSNESS expresses HIMSELF with every Idea that could ever be. (If HE were unexpressed HE would be a wonderful something in the middle of nothing.

3. You and your invisible consciousness are DIVINE CONSCIOUSNESS'S expression of HIMSELF as a compound idea of all right Ideas.

4. When your invisible consciousness stands before the mirror of Truth, the "reflections" are all the material objects or material symbols that you see each day (car, stars in the sky, human body, dental floss, etc). At that starting point your body is a perfect, pain-free reflection of ideas. A compound idea of all right ideas. Then along come the human Beliefs, which mess everything up by causing fear, selfishness, accidents, sickness, hatred, etc.

5. When you are the victim of these Beliefs the best thing you can do is to acknowledge the presence of DIVINE CONSCIOUSNESS as the only Power in

the entire Universe. You have to "ask" HIM to evaporate the Beliefs that have you off balance and are hurting your performance.

Then you stop.

No longwinded appeals. No repetitive rituals. No self-condemnation. Just simply "stop!" Go off and start enjoying yourself. HE will take care of evaporating the threatening BELIEFS. If you can grasp this sequence of events you will be a "happy camper" most every day of your human experience, and have a more than adequate income.

If your relief happens immediately society shouts "Miracle"! If it happens gradually, you alone merely whisper "Thanks". You then have a sense of serenity because you realize "Divine Consciousness" is protecting you.

If you as a teenager traveled this far in the book to be reading this sentence... you have my compliments and respect. You will probably float to the top 95% of whatever occupation you choose, because you had the courage to examine and maybe even think through this controversial subject.

My guess is that the one or two of you out of a 100, that grasped even a portion of what I have brought to your attention, will end up as mayor of your town, as governor of the State you live in, as an astronauts for NASA, as chancellors of a large University, as a Supreme Court justice, and maybe, maybe, maybe as President of your country.

Notes

APPENDIX III
A Good-bye Message
From J.R.

The editors I have worked with on this book have encouraged me to present a biographic accounting of my 70 plus years. My experience probably is as exciting (highs) and as mundane (lows) as every other human being. It is not really important what experiences make up "my story". What is important is what makes up "your story". At the teenage level you have unlimited energy. Even if that energy is misdirected by a miserable home environment or some tragic event that has scared you, you can still blossom into a mature adult. Allow yourself to let it all out and not hold back. So long as you are doing "good" you will be on the right side of the fence, and you will have enough money, a satisfactory soul mate, and the most important thing of all... ***a family to be with.***

People in jail or those who commit suicide most frequently do so because they feel "all-alone" and not a part of any tribe. Even a dysfunctional family, and we all have one or two eccentrics in our immediate family relationships, clings together and accepts all the problems that go with it just for the feeling of "belonging". We all need to be "understood" and the only people who can understand us are those that make up the group we are traveling with. The point I am making is no matter how down you get, you can come out of it by finding some group that will accept you for what you are. When that happens you will get a renewed sense of confidence and the energy will flow as you bubble over with new enthusiasm for living.

You can then allow yourself to see the channel to travel in for financial success. More importantly, try to just enjoy the freedom and exhilaration of being your own person. What I have just described is what has happened to me over my lifetime, and someday, you will be in my position trying to stimulate enthusiastic thinking on the part of your children or grandchildren. It could be that a few comforting words from you will make a big difference in some other persons life, the same as I am trying to make a difference in your life.

If you like what you have read and most of it makes sense to you, consider sharing it with your friends and then selling this book in your neighborhood so you can make a few dollars more per week than working for minimum wage someplace. You can buy this book from me in quantities of five (5) on the Internet at approximately the same price the large bookstores pay. You can then resell the book at the same price for which it is selling in these large bookstores.

What happens is you may no longer have to work behind the counter of a coffee shop listening to people ordering while your legs are so tired you just wish you could sit down. Maybe you can quit your part time job changing oil at the garage and get away from the finger nails that never seem to get clean no matter how often you wash them. Why not make a larger amount of money just riding a bike around your neighborhood knocking on doors (dress with care) asking the occupant if they need a gift for their children or grandchildren for birthdays, graduation, or stocking stuffers for Christmas? If you have read or studied the book, you can tell whoever answers the door what was meaningful to you in the book and how it can enrich the lives of their grandchildren, or children. All of a sudden you are in business for yourself with a product that you are sold on. How about selling the book for $10.00 or more to stores that sell things to teenagers? They can sell it for $15.00 at the check out counter where parents pay the bill. Most every parent wants his or her kids to succeed and this might make a good gift for someone. Consider calling on the owner's of stores that sell high-ticket items such as Jewelry, very expensive autos, Furriers, etc. Suggest to the owner of the store that they can build future business by giving a gift of this book to all purchasers whose sale brings in over $1000 of profit. How about asking your local Realtor to give the book as a gift to their buyers at closing? You must remember to call the first order in yourself so we can register you as the commission sales person for all future purchases from that address. The office or the individual Realtor can put their own advertising stamp or logo on the cover to remind customers they exist for future purchases and referrals. The idea behind giving a gift to wealthy customers is not that they want or need to read the book. They will pass it on to younger people they know, which will make them feel good about themselves. It is the same way your parents feel good about themselves when they give you a gift that is meaningful to you. It makes wealthy people feel good to share or teach younger people to work smart and save money the same way they did to accumulate wealth.

   The idea here is that wealthy buyers understand how to make large sums of money in their own business. Even the mention of the word "millionaire" gets their attention the same way the mere mention of some popular rock band gets your attention. They most likely will probably see the immediate value of having their children or grandchildren read the book. They may even want to read it themselves since it has to do with making a profit and that is almost the only subject they think about all day long anyway.

Consider calling on factories in your neighborhood. Ask the boss if he want to give a book as a Christmas gift to all the employees. The employees would probably like to pass the book onto their children to help them be more financially successful than themselves. Suggest to the boss that the employees might think more highly and give more respect to the boss because the gift directly affects the children of the employee in a favorable manner. Mention to the boss that the employees may then try to pay the boss back, for considering the employee's children and family, by going out of their way to help cut costs or increase production. Everyone wins. It all comes about because you took a chance and invested a small portion of your time without any guarantee of financial success to make the boss aware that the book exists.

This is how you start a business of your own. You test the water with your big toe before you jump in to and find it too cold or too hot. You can try soliciting one or two customers during your lunch hour. If you can sell one customer you can sell a hundred. If you can't sell a single one then back off and continue on with your hourly job.

Imagine how good you are going to feel about yourself when the boss calls you to (make sure you leave a card with your name and phone) reorder. This shows he really appreciates your having stopped in since his employees really liked the idea of having a guide so they could teach their own children how to rise to a higher level of earnings. All of a sudden the not so highly educated factory worker employee becomes a source of knowledge to his own kids. That will probably bring a tear to the eyes of some of those parents who finally feel they have done something for their kids besides just furnishing the bare minimum of food and shelter. Remember, you were the one to put the whole thing in motion. Maybe one of your parents is business oriented and he or she can help you with additional ideas on where to make sales calls in your neighborhood. Maybe the two of you will spend some time together on this project and renew the bond that existed before you went from a child in daddy's lap to an independent teenager.

In a real stretch of imagination, assume this book catches on in the market place. We could possibly form a company with 90% of the employees being teenagers. They could be in cities throughout the world with the main office being Palatine, Illinois. On a part time basis those employed would handle the computers, advertising, and attempt to handle whatever problems came up (adults would take over the problems if they were too large). The idea would be like "Junior Achievement" but with real bullets. It would probably be less than professional and not so profitable, but it would be fun to see 17 year olds having to think on their feet for the first time. Essentially it would be a lab class for those interested in business. Whether profitable or not, if the idea stuck to the wall instead of melting down, imagine the bonding and future travel possibilities for yourself with other kids in Europe, the Mid East, Asia and South America, who were also employees. You would have a contact in another country.

Good results come in many different forms. It could be you won't sell a single book. However, maybe the only success you will have for all your effort to try to help or teach other teenagers is that you could meet the first love of your life in the process of calling on potential buyers. The worst that can happen, if you don't sell a single book, is that you will have books on hand to give as gifts to younger relatives. Another extreme example that might be judged as carrying this whole concept too far is… what if you owned 10 books you could not sell and you just wanted to get rid of them. What if you saw homeless persons on the street or outside a Shelter House? Maybe you would just pass out a few copies for free. Who knows, you might be the cause of the homeless person, who actually reads the book, forgiving themselves for causing the tragedy they feel so guilty about from years ago and they will get a job and rejoin society. You would never find out about it, but if you did such an unselfish act you would feel good about yourself and you would find a way to reward yourself far beyond the few dollars you lost passing out the few books you owned.

Consider sending me e-mail at JR@TheFutureBelongsToMe.com. We can both massage this solicitation concept based on your experiences in the field visiting with a few potential customers. I can then pass any success stories on to other teenagers who are not connecting. Your success story might give them an insight, which will then perpetuate the whole concept of the two rules we started with.

We are now down to the end of what I have to pass onto each of you.

Bear with me as I try to tie everything together so you will have a summary phrase or concept to carry with you for the rest of your life, as follows:

Most authors declare that the following are the major religious groups in the world at the moment in random order and not by importance or size:

Baha'i Faith
Buddhism
Christianity
Confucianism
Contrarianism
Hinduism
Islam
Jainism
Judaism
Native Spirituality
Sikhism
Taoism
Zoroastrianism

Every one of the above is different in the rituals that they use to worship. However, everyone of them is exactly the same regarding their basic mission statement to their parishioners..." Do unto others as you would have others do unto you".

This mission statement of "Do Unto Others..." is the short way of saying *"You can't help someone else without helping yourself"* and "the more you give the more you get" which is where we began the book.

Enough has now been said and it is time to turn out the lights and settle in.

"Good night and Good luck."

Edward R. Murrow, a columnist of the 1960 era, made this phrase famous by saying it to sign off his radio show

J.R. - John Ratkovich
JR@TheFutureBelongsToMe.com
www.TheFutureBelongsToMe.com to order books.

Notes

Guía de los adolescentes a convertirse en un millonario
El futuro pertenece a mí!

Por J.R.

AGRADECIMIENTOS Y RECONOCIMIENTOS

A todos los adolescentes y adultos sofisticados que han contribuido a las varias revisiones de este libro, los elogio por ayudarme a hacerlo posible.

Agradezco especialmente a mi vecina, Pamela Parsons, escritora y editora de North Barrington, Illinois, quien pasó muchas horas contribuyendo con sus críticas constructivas al arreglo y la estructura del libro. Le recomiendo a cualquier persona que necesite consejo para escribir un libro, que se dirija a: aromaticthymes@mac.com

Agradecemos la colaboración de Sue Kramer de Eagle Press, Crystal Lake, Illinois, quien nos dio ideas para cautivar la imaginación de un joven. sue@eaglepresscl.net

Especial agradecimiento a Beatrice Sanguino (beasanguino@gmail.com) por su exactitud en la traducción de este libro al español. El lector podrá juzgar la calidad al comparar las dos ediciones y en el futuro en Francés y alemán.

Un agradecimiento especial a Julie Salisbury por su conocimiento de saber qué editorial estara más intersado en su tema. Si eres un autor principiante considera contactarla a contact@inspiresbook.com.

Un agradecimiento especial a Trace Krug por su contribución en el trabajo de arte de la cubertura del libro – TraceK@sbcglobal.net y tambien a Justin Sachs al www.JSachs.com.

GUÍA PARA EL ADOLESCENTE: CÓMO CONVERTIRSE EN MILLONARIO

By J.R

El Futuro Me Pertenece!

TABLA DE CONTENIDO

"Introducción"

Volver al futuro 1
¡Este libro fue escrito para ti! 3
Mantener tu interés 8

Capitulo Uno
"Vuela como un águila"

¡Tú puedes lograrlo! 9
Autorízate a ser rico 9
El sentido de todo 12

Capitulo Dos
"La carne del libro"

Las reglas de batalla 15
¿Por qué funcionan las dos reglas? 18
Patentas Complejos 23
Diagrama De Apoyo - Creencias v. Ideas 27
Padres 30
Empezar hoy 31
Que afortunado eres 34
Enséñame el dinero 35
Igual que en las películas de vaqueros 37

Capítulo Tres
"Las cosas prácticas"

Tu primer trabajo de tiempo completo 39
Ropa 40
Cómo no conseguir el empleo 43
Pagar por tu disfraz 45

Capítulo Cuatro
"*Tus elecciones Personales*"

Dar órdenes o recibir órdenes 47
Sé tú mismo 50
Perdónate 51
Reservas de dinero 55
Logra que otra persona pague tu universidad 55
En tu propio vecindario 58

Capítulo Cinco
"Consejos útiles a medida que maduras"

Consejos Emparesariales 65
Algunos Ejemplos 65
Los análisis por ecrito 67
Consejos personales: La relación chico-chica 68
Resoluer el problema entre los sexos 70
Varias reglas para los hombres 70
Varias reglas par alas mujeres 72
Dos tenedores y un pastel .72
Tratar con un acosador 73
Record Criminal 75
Sexting, mensajes de texto y los actos delictivos 76

Capítulo Seis
"Referencias"

Lecturas seleccionadas 85
Vestir para tener exito 85
Fuente para ropa hecha a medida 86
Acciones especulativas seleccionadas 87
Fuentes de monedas de oro y plata o ETFs 89
Beca de caddie para la Universidad 90
Macrobióteca 90
El reconocimiento de las nuevas
   industrias millionarias 91

Capítulo Siete
"Mas allá de nuestras fronteras"

Adolescentes en otros países 93

Capítulo Ocho
"Resumen"

El futuro 97

Capítulo Nueve
"Epilogo"

Guía para el Millonario:
cómo volver a ser un Adolescente 99
Mi próximo libro 99
Universidad de Millonarios .99

Capítulo Diez
"Páginas de Crecimiento Personal"

Metas 103
Sugerencias a conciderar para mejorar 104
Fuentes de inversiones potenciales 105
¡Felicitaciones! 107

Apéndice

Breve explicación sobre metafísica 109

Apéndice Dos

Un mensaje de despedida por J.R. 111

Prólogo

"Muchos adultos de 35 años, que actualmente viven de cheque a cheque, recuerdan la preparatoria y lamentan el no haber tenido un adulto experimentado que los guiara para llegar a ser ricos".

La idea principal, la cual te da ganancias es la que tú te recompensas porque te sientes bien contigo mismo.

> *"En América, toda ave es libre de sentarse en cualquier árbol"*
>
> *– Anónimo*

Introducción
"Volver Al Futuro"

Hola estudiantes: aquí es donde empezamos nuestro viaje. Imagínate que te encuentras en tu habitación al terminar el día. Durante la próxima hora, acomódate para un emocionante, entretenido y educativo viaje imaginario a tu futuro. Mi sugerencia es que leas toda la sección de Inglés o Español en una sentada. Toma un lápiz amarillo o rojo y marca los párrafos que te interesen en cada capítulo.

Cuando estes al final del libro, tu puedes escojer a lo que quieres regresar y vas a ver que este libro está diseñado para uso continuo. No es un libro de "una ves" y despues se guarda. Te voy a dar 54 años de lo que yo he aprendido siendo un padre de 3 hijos y 3 hijas y 9 nietos. Debe de haber algo en este libro qué te puede traer más certeza a tus años de adolescencia y evaporar algunas anciedades que cada uno tiene.

Imagínate como un hombre o mujer adulto y hazte la siguiente pregunta: "Cada mañana al amanecer, ¿quiero ver el océano desde el balcón en el piso décimo de mi condominio en Hawai (o Florida) o quiero estar preparándome para mi viaje a la fábrica local de Chicago o Los Ángeles, donde estaré metiendo mi tarjeta de ingreso en una máquina, al empezar mi día?"

Un número limitado de personas vienen a este mundo con talentos para música, teatro, ó deportes. Estas personas reciben gran cantidad de dinero por exhibir sus talentos ante otras personas. ¡Después estamos el resto de nosotros! Tenemos padres típicos, una crianza normal y eventualmente nos graduamos de la preparatoria o Universidad. Ahora tenemos que encontrar un trabajo de tiempo completo.

La idea de tener una carrera que realmente nos satisfaga en vez de simplemente trabajar lo suficiente para ganar dinero y así vivir al día, es el enfoque de todos nosotros. Sin embargo, hasta que no estés seguro de cuál carrera elegir, o cuál será tu especialidad, ¿por qué no hacer que tu carrera simplemente sea ganar todo el dinero que tú puedas en un corto plazo de tiempo? Con este razonamiento flexible, cuando cumplas 35 años de edad, podrás tener más dinero en el banco que lo que jamás podrías gastar. Si esta idea hace las delicias de tu paladar, entonces ponte cómodo y revisemos cada sección de este libro párrafo por párrafo.

¡Este Libro Fue Escrito Para Ti!

Se han escrito muchos libros sobre "Cómo convertirse en millonario?" para inversionistas adultos, pero existen pocos libros para los jóvenes. Este libro fue escrito para ti – un joven en la preparatoria que probablemente nunca ha pensado en lo que estará haciendo dentro de unos años para alimentarse.

Yo he observado a un extenso número de jóvenes que se enfocan en gastar mucho su dinero en artículos como boletos de conciertos y ropa de la última moda. La idea de ser ahorrativo y reducir tus hábitos de gastos – para cuando tengas los 35 años de edad, tu cuenta bancaria tendrá más dinero que el que tú y tu familia jamás hayan imaginado –posiblemente sería muy "fuera de serie" para muchos de ustedes. Sin embargo, quizás tú eres "especial". Quizás tú eres único y sobresalgas sobre la muchedumbre. Quizás tú eres unos de los pocos jóvenes que tienen la suficiente madurez a una edad temprana y toman mis sugerencias en serio.

Tómate una pausa por un momento. Nota que recientemente has empezado a pensar en tu futuro, ahora que posiblemente estés disfrutando de haber conocido tu primer amor en tu escuela o en tu vecindario. También puede ser que un punto de vista nuevo repentinamente te haya llevado de la niñez a la semi-madurez. Considera permitirte absorber el significado de las ideas que se encuentran dentro de este libro como los cimientos sobre cuales puedes construir y asegurar tu futuro financiero para tu familia o tu profesión.

Observa a tu Mamá y tu Papá. Posiblemente sean bastante exitosos en sus carreras y puede parecer que con poco esfuerzo te brindan un hogar cálido y también satisfacen todas tus necesidades materiales. Sin embargo, algunos de ustedes tienen padres que no hablan inglés muy bien, otros no recibieron una educación adecuada para obtener un empleo bien remunerado, o quizás vivan con el temor de perder su trabajo o ser suspendidos. Posiblemente tú seas víctima de un ambiente hogareño que sufre su porción de problemas tales como la falta de un padre o madre, o quizás problemas más serios. Probablemente te sientas "siempre solo"; muchos de ustedes se encuentran en estas situaciones. Sin embargo, algunas de las sugerencias de este libro te darán una nueva dirección para que tú mismo puedas asumir un mayor control sobre tu vida personal.

¿Porqué he escrito este libro?

Mi hipótesis inicial era que los adolescentes le importa un bledo mi motivación para escribir este libro.

Entonces mientras toda la edición y corrección de pruebas estaba en procesp, los profesionales que me asistían seguian animándome para contar mi"historia" sin echarme a llorar cuando la contara.

Yo seguia pendado que fue "el evento" que se produjo para obtener todo el proceso en funcionamiento sería muy aburrido para cualquier adolescente. Entonces me dijeron que a todo el mundo le gusta escuchar la historia detrás de la escena. Pregunté alrededor mio y por supuesto la curiosidad es na fuerte poderosa del motivación.

La bombilla se encendión de repente en mi mente.

Vi donde ustedes los adolescents deben ser consientes de

cómo una sola experiencia en su futuro (tan pronto como mañana) podría precipitar un talento con el cual has nacido. En la actualidad, quizás te guste dibujar dibujos animdos, aviones del futuro, ropa y joyas para damas. Quizás te guste contar chistes ridiculos o historias de perros peludos que causan mucha risa. A lo mejor eres el payaso de tu clase, o quizás seas muy coordinado con las manos y los ojos en una tabla de skate.

Cuando demuestres cualquier talento natural y superior que tengas todos los dias, probablemente ni siguiera estás altanto del potencial de ese regalo. Tú probablemente nunca has visto tus habilidades especiales como algo del otro mundo o como una forma de ganarte una fortuna y recibir satisfacción personal. Un dia en el futuro, mientras estás bromeando con tus amigos, alguien dice "oye, Juan o Maria, verdaderamente tienes un talento. ¿Por qué no creas algo con ello?"

Eso fue lo que me pasó a los 70 años de edad. Esperemos que a ti te pueda pasar antes.

Un profesor de segundaria a Taft High School en el noreste de Chicago me llamó por telefono un dia para preguntarme si yo podria hacer un discurso en el dia de la carrera.

El mismo dia que tenia que hacer mi discurso, me vesti con un traje de tres piezas, camisa blanca y corbata roja, este es mi vestuario de cada dia en mi oficina.

Ahora la trama se complica: yo no tenia la menor idea de que hablar. Solo el dia anterior me pidieron de hacer un discurso. Aparentemente alguien tuvo una emergencia y yo tenia que remplazar a esa persona. Pensé en preguntar a los estudiantes cual era el tema de moda en el campus y improvisar a partir de ahi.

Los estudiantes de 17-18 años llenaron las aulas y cuando ya estaban todos sentados, el profesor nos presentó a mi y a otro que tambien haria un discurso.

Yo era el primero que tenia que hacer el discurso. Justo cuando estaba a punto de empezar, entrá un muchacho con aspecto de atleta, muy deportista. El profesor le pregunto si llegaba tarde porque habia estado en las otras aulas escuchando los discursos.

El se sento muy cómodo el la silla más lejana a donde me encontraba yo y alzo una pierna en el escritorio. Su descripción de los oradores de las ortras aulas fue que "no vale nada." Entonces preguntó que porque las escuelas hacen que los estudiates desperdicien su tiempo escuchando a gente ajena hablar de lo que hacen todos los dias en el trbajo. Lo que dijo el joven tenia sentido para mi.

Empezé a hacer preguantas sobre el tema de moda de estos dias en la escuela y cada uno dijo algo sobre ello. En el momento apropiado, utilize, lo que uno de los estudiantes dijo y aprovenché para hablar sobre mi objetivo...quien quiere ganar un montón de dinero? Entonces dije que ser rico no es nada vergonzoso. Hablé sobre las dos reglas "dar mas de lo que recibes asi recibes más de lo que das" y "no puedes ayudar a alguien sin ayudarte a ti primero." Hubo un leve intercamvio de ideas entre los estudiantes. La sesión acabó y el profesor preguntó a las estudiantes si tenian alguna preguanta. Nadie contestó.

El profesor me dio las gracias por mi discurso y era obvio que la sesión habia terminado. Fue entonces cuando el joven de aspecto atleta, el que estaba sentado en la parte trasera de la aula, se levantó y empezó a aplaudir muy, muy lentamente con una pausa de un o dos segundoes entre cada aplauso. Me esta mirando fijamente a los ojos. Dejó de aplaudir y sin una palabra se acercó a mi fijandome bien a álos ojos y sacudió la barbilla asi como hacen los guerreros en las peliculas despues de haber ganado la batalla para darse "reconocimiento" el uno al otro por haber sobrevivido. Despues desaparecio en el pasillo con los otros estudiantes.

Eso me tocó en la mas profundo de mi ser. No puedo recordar jamás en mis 70 años de edad haberme sentido tan emocional, abrumando, y temporalmente desenfocadó.

Fue esa noche que empezé a escribir este libro porque algunas de las ideas que presenté le tocaron a ese joven. Si ese joven vio el sentido en mis palabras, en lo que yo intentaba decir, entonces tenia yo que mandar ese mensaje a otro jovenes.

Final de la historia. Espero que entiendas lo que estaba tratando de trasmitir. Tú tambien tendras una experincia asi algun dia en tu vida. Cuando te ocurrá, acuerdate de mi y sige con ello. "Sé todo lo que puedes ser" con el talento con el cúal has nacido. No te detengas. Ese será "tú" momento.

Mantener tu interés

He limitado el ámbito a lo que estas a punto de leer porque pensé que sería mejor tener algo breve y atractivo en vez de un libro escolar que trata de ser todo para todo el mundo.

Sólo me referiré un poco a cómo invertir dinero, puesto que existen muchos libros en la biblioteca que te ayudarán con eso o simplemente puedes buscar información sobre el tema en Internet. Muchos de ustedes deberían poder acabar este libro en solo una lectura. Si desean escribirme con sugerencias sobre cómo elaborar o mejorar los temas que menciono, envíen su correspondencia a:

America Home Finance, Inc
830 W Northwest Highway
Palatine, Illinois 60067

Por el contrario, si desean tener un diálogo conmigo, pueden hacerlo a través de mi correo electrónico:

JR@TheFutureBelongsToMe.com

Contestaré sus preguntas tal como he hecho y hago todavía con mis propios hijos.

Capítulo Uno
"Vuela como un águila"

"Cualquier persona que haya luchado contra la pobreza sabe bien lo caro que es ser pobre."
-Anónimo

¡Tú puedes lograrlo!

Este capítulo apunta a que comiences a pensar sobre la opción de quedarte estancado o avanzar.

Imagínate qué dirían tus parientes si tú anunciaras: "voy hacer mi carrera de millonario". Puesto que algunos están viviendo de cheque a cheque, posiblemente te ignoren. Otros quizás se rían para sus adentros. Algunos te criticarán debido a su envidia y su propia inseguridad. El simple hecho de pensar que tú ganarás más dinero en un solo año, cuando ellos tienen 20 años luchando, puede ocasionar que se ofendan.

Muchos de tus familiares te quieren y te respetan, y admiran tus aspiraciones. Sin embargo, si algunos familiares o adultos te dicen que no vayas más allá de conseguir un trabajo y trabajar para otro durante los próximos 40 años, pregúntate: ¿qué han logrado ellos en su vida? ¿Qué tan calificados están para desanimarme y detenerme en el desarrollo de todo mi potencial? ¿Manejan ellos un Honda oxidado o un Mercedes Benz lujoso?

Autorízate a ser rico

Voy a asumir desde el principio que tú te das cuenta de que en América tienes la libertad de escoger ser millonario así como tienes el derecho a llegar a ser un nadador que compita en las Olimpíadas, ganar un Golden Globe, o ser nominado para Juez de la Corte Suprema, o escoger una carrera apropiada. Desagamos de cualguier concepto negativo que hay algo incorrecto en ser adinerado.

Se conoce a América como la tierra de las oportunidades. Quizás hayas leído en el periódico noticias sobre inmigrantes ilegales que arriesgan sus vidas para entrar a los Estados Unidos de América: ellos se quieren quedar aquí porque nuestro sistema les da la oportunidad de lograr sus sueños económicos si se rigen por nuestras leyes vigentes. Considera darte la libertad de expresarte y darle a todas tus ideas una oportunidad. Existe el rumor de que el actor estadounidense Harrison Ford era sólo un carpintero que trabajaba en la escenografía original de la película Star Wars I antes de ensayar para la parte de un piloto sabelotodo: la película ganó el premio Oscar.

Cuando tú veas una oportunidad, actúa. No dejes que la oportunidad te pase por alto y te deje con las manos vacías. Es igual cuando te esfuerzas por crear una nueva página en la red mundial o tratas de vender algo en tu vecindario simplemente para probar cuánto logras. Cuando dudes, considera correr un riesgo para que en el futuro no te arrepientas y, al mirar hacia atrás no te preguntes qué hubiera sucedido si hubieras aprovechado la oportunidad.

Esto puede ser dificil para muchos adolescents porque tus amigos sercanos probablemente te van a desanimar de explorer tus nuevas ideas porque ellos no aprecian o entienden la prevision que tu tienes. ¿Entonces que haces? Tu encuetras un lugar calmado y empienzas a escribir tus ideas. Despues del tiempo tu vas a tener un sentimiento positive o negative y vas a continuar o parar con tus ideas. En cualquier caso – tu lo intentaste.

Por ejemplo

Deberías viajar a Alaska para trabajar en la pesca del verano o simplemente trabajar en el taller de bicicleta de tu pueblo hasta que algo mejor venga.

Aquí presento un ejercicio sencillo para ayudarte cuando se presente una oportunidad:

Al igual que cuando te sugerí al empezar, cierra tus ojos sólo por un momento ¿Qué pensamientos vienen a tu mente? Si te viene a la mente el sexo opuesto, entonces sigue con esa visión. La visión es la llave para abrir la puerta al dinero, sólo hace. Por ejemplo, en qué productos piensan las mujeres jóvenes? Posiblemente tú puedas mejorar ese producto o inventar uno completamente nuevo. Si tu visión es sobre los deportes o cualquier otro logro, trata de que tu mente corra sin obstáculo y explore nuevas IDEAS. Quizás te imagines inventando un nuevo lápiz de labios o perfume, o un papel sensible al calor que en vez de escribir sobre él con un lápiz o una pluma, simplemente se marque con el dedo. Tu trabajo debe ser descubrir cuál buena IDEA está frente a ti. Cuando sientas un alto nivel de confianza, actúa.

Descubrirás que estos ejercicios te ayudarán cuando ya estés en tus años mayores; las decisiones que tomas tienen gran importancia para tu futuro. Tu trabajo es DESCUBRIR lo que es correcto para ti, NO CREARLO. Crearlo le toca al jefe. Recuerda, cada tribu sobre este planeta denomina al jefe con diferentes nombres, pero él o ella ya saben cuál sería la mejor búsqueda para ti en determinado momento. ¡Por lo tanto, este ejercicio es una buena manera de enfocarte en lo que fue creado especialmente para ti!

Regresemos a la meta de autorizarte a crearte una carrera para hacer dinero. Ser millonario no es nada especial. Simplemente significa que tienes más dinero para gastar en comparación a muchos a tu alrededor. Por sí solo, el dinero no te hace una mejor persona. Tus héroes del deporte, tus ídolos de los conciertos, tu médico familiar y otros hombres y mujeres adinerados son personas ordinarias igual que tú. Ellos probablemente pasaron las mismas experiencias en la escuela con los mismo altibajos que tú experimentarás. Ellos simplemente escojieron -o calleron- en una carrera que era aproriada para tus habilidades intelectuales o físicas,y ganar mucho dinero usando estas facultades.

Tú también tienes el derecho de llegar a hacer lo mismo en cualquier rama que escojas, y así podrás ganar mucho dinero – más de lo que puedas gastar – sencillamente siguiendo las sugerencias que se encuentran en este libro hasta que una se te haga más clara carrera exitosa.

Permítete dejar que tu mente desarrolle la habilidad de ganar dinero de la misma manera en la que entrenarías tu cuerpo para memorizar un ejercicio de kárate. Las ideas que se encuentran en este libro te darán un esquema o plan para ayudarte a empezar. Después podrás modificar lo que te he sugerido de acuerdo a tus necesidades personales. Si sientes que no captas o no entiendes el significado de lo que te sugiero, entonces toma un descanso en la lectura de este libro, ya que todavía no estás lo suficiente maduro para esta disciplina. Con el tiempo podrás lograrlo. Cuando sientas que algo está bien para ti,entonces comprenderás lo que te estoy diciendo.

El sentido de todo

Para tú que tomas este libro en serio: mi objetivo es convertirte en millonario, no porque tengas un talento especial por el cual una audiencia pagaría mucho dinero, sino porque has demostrado talento porque has desarrollado la habilidad de ver con los ojos y oír con los oídos. Ver con los ojos y oír con los oídos significa que tú trabajas con los talentos que tienes a mano. Aprovéchate de tus habilidades y no te sientas inferior porque no eressúper atleta ó modelo de vestido de talla 4. Quizás algunos jóvenes inventen una nueva computadora, mientras tú puedes inventar un nuevo lema para una camiseta o un diseño nuevo de vestido. Tú puedes alzar la cabeza porque tu creatividad están a la par de las otras personas. La opinión que tú tienes de ti mismo es lo único que importa. Si tú no aceptas este concepto nunca podrás desarrollarte a tu potencial completo.

Todos ustedes, si tienen una inteligencia constante, pueden enfocarse con disciplina a la meta de ser millonario. Todavía pueden ingresar al Peace Corps, que no paga mucho. Todavía pueden ser millonarios en su tiempo libre trayendo nuevas ideas a un país del Tercer Mundo que estén visitando. Después de todo, solamente hay algunas horas en el día en que puedes trabajar para otra persona mientras desarrollas tu propio negocio. Muchos de ustedes son demasiado jóvenes para darse permiso para ser un millonario y los miembros de tu familia no están pensando sobre el tema: entonces alguien tiene que motivarte. Este libro es tu permiso para lograr una carrera para ser millonario. Si aprendes estas lecciones bien, algún día en el futuro cercano les darás a tus hijos e hijas el mismo permiso de desarrollar su potencial completo en cualquier carrera que escojan.

Notes

Capítulo Dos
"La carne del libro"

"Aunque seas rico o pobre, es mejor tener dinero."

Las reglas de batalla

Existen dos reglas que me gustaría que memorice para convertirte en millonario:

- La primera regla es "Cuanto más des, más recibirás."
- La segunda regla es "No puedes ayudar a otra persona sin ayudarte a ti mismo."

Todo adulto millonario que esté leyendo este libro y haya ganado su fortuna legalmente, reconocerá lo que digo.

Sospecho que algunos estarán haciendo gestos sobre el consejo de dar y luego recibir, pero el resultado de las dos reglas mencionadas será sentirte bien contigo mismo. El sentirse bien con uno mismo es una formula primordial en todos los aspectos de nuestra vida. Cuando te sientes bien contigo mismo, tu estima y tu confianza en ti mismo son elevadas. A la vez, tu intuición y el nivel de habilidad que tienes parecen aumentar y ves las cosas más claramente. Descubrirás que puedes tomar buenas decisiones financieras en el momento apropiado, tales como comprar acciones en la bolsa o comprar de bienes raíces.

Si practicas deporte, en béisbol sería el día que, como lanzador, no permitas que el otro equipo batee la pelota, o en fútbol americano que logres el bloqueo perfecto, o en competiciones de gimnasio que logres puntuación perfecta, o

Notes

correr 200 metros en sólo 21, 74 segundos. Para las mujeres jóvenes, quizás diseñes un vestido perfecto para esa ocasión especial o quizás te desempeñes mejor que nunca como actriz, música, académica, o en tu caballo. Es como una "liberación" emocional. Cuando simplemente te dejas llevar, en vez de ser temeroso o vacilante, suceden cosas maravillosas.

Cuando tú "das de ti más de lo que recibes" generalmente tiene lugar la siguiente reacción: de 10 personas a quienes tú haces el bien (o sea algo fuera de lo ordinario donde no te era obligatorio hacer algo por la persona o ser tan generoso con tu tiempo o dinero), uno de ellos verá tus esfuerzos como una señal de debilidad que puede ser aprovechada. Esa persona probablemente trate de aprovecharse de ti, lo que te costará emocionalmente o financieramente. (El lado bueno de esto es que ahora sabes que no se puede confiar en nadie). En este ejemplo, cuando alguien se aproveche de ti, tienes que asimilar el golpe y distanciarte. Sin embargo, ocho personas de cada diez te dirán cosas placenteras y será un pequeño logro emocional. El último de los diez estará súper agradecido contigo y dirá elogios que no se pueden comprar con oro ni con diamantes. Tú te sentirás tan bien contigo mismo que hasta brotarán lágrimas de tus ojos y sentirás un calor interno por la satisfacción de haber hecho algo sin egoísmo hacia tu prójimo.

Por sentirte tan bien lograrás una especie de elevación, en la que eres más apto para tomar buenas decisiones financieras, entre otras cosas.

Muchos de tus profesores, dentro o fuera de tu escuela, experimentan regularmente estas tres reacciones de su estudiantes. Les da una satisfacción tremenda ver que uno de ustedes alcance su potencial completo en lo académico y, en un sentido, logran ser millonarios en educación, guiándolos para hacer del mundo un mejor lugar. La única razón por la que tus maestros no han buscado diamantes y dinero afuera de su carrera es porque han optado por no hacerlo. Algunas personas pueden ser ricas por haber recibido un herencia o por haber inventado algo, o por haber invertido en apartamentos, pero la mayoría de tus maestros ven los logros de sus estudiantes con más importancia que los logros económicos que ellos puedan lograr jamás. Con los maestros que admires, considera fijarte en su mirada la próxima vez que tengas una conversación privada o en un grupo y, con sinceridad, dale las "Gracias".

¿Por qué funcionan las dos reglas?

Tengo que explicar lo que mencioné en los últimos párrafos. Las cosas buenas no siempre vienen hacia ti sólo porque seas generoso y hayas ayudado a alguien. Lo que sucede es que te sientes tan bien contigo mismo que tus temores o tus incertidumbres personales temporalmente se evaporan de tu mente (temor, coraje, venganza, culpabilidad, etc.). El resultado es que de repente aparecen frente a ti IDEAS buenas y brillantes, como un campo de flores en primavera y tú tienes el derecho a recolectar todas las flores que necesites.

Alguna vez pensaste de adonde viene la palabra ARCA. Varias personas dicen que es el nombre del bote que sobrevivió 40 días y noches de lluvia que inundo la tierra. Considera la palabra ARCA de un significado de un acto de bondad. Considera que el mito del bote es un mensaje para salvarte tu mismo por un acto de bondad que te borra la mente y te pone en "la zona". Este acto de bondad es la vida del bote. Los animales en el ARCA son las miles de ideas que tú ves cuando la mente se borra por 40 segundos o 40 días de cosas que no son importante. La lluvia es la purga de tu mente de las creencias que están ahogadas por el sentimiento bueno en ti mismo. Entonces cuando te recompensas mentalmente por "ir con" o explorar una o más de tus ideas tu vas a terminar en éxito financiero. No es importante que el ARCA existiera o que era una fabula para incentivar un comportamiento altruista. Lo importante es que cada lector entienda como usar comportamiento altruista para lograr éxito financiero.

Aquí está un ejemplo de mi yerno, quien tiene un entendimiento razonable que distingue bien entre las IDEAS y CREENCIAS: él solucionó un problema que estaba molestando a sus hijos, por el cual probablemente ganará mucho dinero al registrar una patente para proteger su invención.

Mi yerno tiene dos hijas pequeñas a las que les gusta dibujar con marcadores de colores. Sus hijas perdían los tapones de los marcadores debajo de los muebles y los marcadores entonces se secaban, la hija de tres años no tenía suficiente fuerza para quitar el tapón de los marcadores, y también le preocupaba que ella pudiera meterse el tapón en

la boca y asfixiarse.Él muestra una generosidad hacia todos. Él estaba tratando de ayudar a alguien más, siguiendo la segunda regla que consideramos: "No puedes ayudar a alguien sin ayudarte a ti mismo". Su mente se deshizo de CREENCIAS (temor, frustración, irritación, etc.) y pudo ver con claridad la respuesta al problema. La respuesta siempre había estado frente a él, pero no la podía ver, pues estaba nublado por sus CREENCIAS.

Su solución: ¡En vez de poner un tapón en el marcador, pon el marcador en el tapón! Tomó la caja de marcadores y adhirió con pegamento los tapones a la caja, boca abajo. Los niños pequeños ahora podían introducir el marcador en su tapón haciendo fuerza porque tenían un superficie más grande que podían agarrar bien con sus manos pequeñas. Los niños estaban más contentos por tener marcadores que no estaban secos y su papá está en conversaciones con la compañía fabricante de estos marcadores para entablar negocios.

Como trató de ayudar al prójimo, su mente estaba clara, al igual que una tormenta limpia el cielo del polvo y te permite apreciar las estrellas en la noche. Considera tomar riesgos. Ensaya este concepto con circunstancias que pienses pueden ser mejoradas. Dentro de ese esfuerzo, estás ayudando automáticamente al prójimo – incluso cuando aparentemente sólo te estás ayudando a ti mismo. Al permitir que tu mente explore nuevos territorios, aparecerán IDEAS nuevas dentro de ti, entrarás automáticamente en una elevación emocional y las soluciones a tus problemas se te harán obvias.

Por ejemplo: Quien sabe, quizás tú encontrarás una manera de tomar una servilleta de papel, adherirle una capa de plástico por un lado (para proteger tu camisa al comer) y venderla a McDonalds como un babero desechable para comer hamburguesas o bebidas mientras uno conduce un coche. O quizás encuentres la forma de adherir un pegamento a un lado de las toallas de papel en rollo, de forma que una empresa pueda exhibir un anuncio. Imagínate deshacerse de tanto desperdicio de servilletas que la gente tira sin usar. Aquí estarías inventando un babero para comer que se cuelga a tu camisa y se remueve sin esfuerzo dejando tu camisa limpia. Quizás sólo veas a esta idea como otra idea egoísta, pero en realidad estás ayudando a una industria entera, incluyendo a las personas que buscan la conservación de los bosques y selvas.

Qué tal si encuentras la forma de deshacerse de las manchas de chocolate en la ropa y las manos mientras uno consume un helado de chocolate? Considera hacer una envoltura de plástico que al retirarla del helado se desenvuelve como un plátano, y que un lado de la envoltura sea absorbente como una servilleta para absorber el chocolate. Una idea sencilla, pero bastante complicada de concebir.

¿Qué sucedería si te ganas el agradecimiento eterno de esposos agotados y aburridos que tienen que asistir ferias de arte en la calle durante todo el verano? Tienen que mantenerse parados frente a los puestos de los comerciantes mientras sus parejas estudian cada joya o taza de café. ¿Por qué no diseñar una silla que se pueda colocar sobre los postes de luz o teléfono que se encuentran frente a estos puestos? Esto también podría hacer posible que mujeres embarazadas puedan asistir a estas ferias u otras exhibiciones, sabiendo que tendrán donde sentarse ocasionalmente.

Si el profesor de taller en la escuela secundaria puede ayudarte con el diseño, tu podrías fijar el precio del diseño con la empresa local que hace estampados metálicos. A continuación, puedes hacer una cita con el gerente del departamento de planificación de la cuidad en que vives y presentar la idea que se utilizará en todos las areas touristicas o sitios como la feria de verano. El punto de venta sería que el alcalde de tu ciudad podria conseguir publicidad y tal vez conseguir más votos hacia la reelección porque él o ella estaba tratando de hacer algo para el público. Tu ganas una cantidad de dinero como intermediario con la fabricación que es hecha por personas que ya están en el negocio. ¡Todo el mundo gana!

Si usted tiene una idea que crees que tiene la novedad suficiente para justificar una patente considere ponerte en contacto conmigo a **JR@TheFutureBelongsToMe.com**. Yo te daré mi mejor consejo en ese momento.

Mi última hoja probaly se caerá mi árbol en otros 10-12 años, así que no estoy buscando robar las ideas patentables de cualquier persona y causar agravación con la ley.

Quien sabe, tal vez podemos empezar un blog de adolescentes para hablar de nuevo ideas para las patentes. La prueba de que la idea originarial fue tuya, en primer lugar sería en la fecha del blog y esto retrasaría cualquier otra persona de manera flagrante el robo de su idea. Tú tendría que realizar copias con dibujos o prototipos para mostrar la primera vez que tú comenzaste a trabajar en el proyecto.

Podemos limitarla a solamente los adolescentes y desarrollar la idea en un tipo de competencia con algún tipo de premio una vez al año para la mejor idea.

Incluso si no proceden con esto, recuerden lo que usted acaba de leer aquí. Este enfoque extravagante de usar sus ojos para ver y sus oídos oír es lo que te dará el motivo para levantarte de la cama cada mañana con un "chasquido". Esto hace una razón interesante para llegar a la escuela o para hacer algo nuevo. Seguro que es mejor que arraste a ti mismo al baño para iniciar otro día aburrido.

Probablemente me estoy repitiendo, pero permitete ver todos los objetos en tu alrededor y ver si hay espacio para mejorar. Un ejemplo de lo que estoy hablando es el café que usted toma en Starbucks. Hace unos años una persona de su edad tenía dificultad manteniendo la taza de café y tratando de envolver las servilletas alrededor de la taza para proteger las mano contra el calor. El volvió a su casa y inventó el cartón delgado que está actualmente en uso. El probablemente vendió la idea a Starbucks y probablemente le pagaron un centavo por cada uno que compran o usan. Probablemente se gana varios millones de dólares de las patentes.

¿Por qué tú no inventas una manera de poner un plástico en el interior de un frasco de vidrio de mantequilla de maní? La hélice se adjunta a la parte inferior de la tapa y cada vez que se atornilla o se desatornilla el tapón, se mezcle la mantequilla de maní. Esto evitaría el trabajo difícil de usar un cuchillo para remover la mantequilla de maní antes de usarla.

Si realmente quieres ser creativo por qué no hacer el frasco de mantequilla de maní de plástio para que de esa manera tú pudieras masajar o apriete la botella para mezclar el aceite del maní. Una vez que este mezclado, se puede quitar la tapa para usar solamente la cantidad que deseas. Con cualquiera de estas ideas serias el "gran hombre o una mujer en el campus" por un período de tiempo.

Ten en cuenta que para asegurar una patente necesitas una nueva idea con una novedad especial para que la oficina de patentes lo aprueben. Pienses por un momento en los conceptos de la hélice o el frasco. Qual de estas ideas te golpea tener la mejor novedad que sea diferente de cualquier cosa que tú puedes ver en la repisa de una tienda hoy.

Patentas Complejos

Aquí hay una idea para una patente para los que estudian ingeniería. ¿Cuántas veces has perdido tú dominio de una barra de jabón en la ducha y después de caer la barra tuviste que lidiar con los pedasos quebrados y la demora en salir de la ducha?

Has un experimento y toma una barra de jabón, cortala en 4-5 secciones de 1-2 pulgadas. Consigete un plato taza de café de la cocina y pon los pedasos en la taza con suficiente agua para cubrir el plato. Al día siguiente tira el agua y observa la superficie lisa del jabón y los bordes dentados en la parte superior.

Los bordes dentados son para mejor dominio de la barra de jabón y el lado liso es para el uso contra el cuerpo. Tu puedes obtener un derecho por 3 años con la oficina de las patentes pero eso no te va dar tu fortuna.

Como ingeniero tienes que encontrar la manera de construir la maquinaria o las herramientas que se adapten al dia presente. Esta es una idea patentable que pues vender a la compañia de jabón o depronto tu y tu padre pueden empezar un taller y tu padre va tener un programa de jubilación que nadie se lo puede quitar. Esta será su manera de pagarle a tú padre de vuelta por todo el amor y el cuidado que te ha dado en el pasado.

Si tú vas a cualquier desconocido para obtener ayuda con esta idea, entoces tu deves de tener una declaración por escrito que simplemente dice que tu ablaste con ellos en ese día en particular sobre la idea de "diseño de una máquina o herramientas para la fabricación de una bara de jabón con un lado liso para la piel y un lado dentado para mayor agarre con la mano", esto te asegura un 90% que la idea no va ser robada por la 3ª persona. Me gustaría ser su primer cliente al realizar la producción. Consideran que el nombre sera "jabón de las Montañas Rocky".

El siguiente es un ejemplo de lo que estoy hablando, tomado de www.About.com.

En 1994 Kathryn Gregory, ahora una adolescente de Bedford, Massachusetts, se convirtió en una inventora y una empresariaa la edad de diez años. De acuerdo de "Wristies", "un día frío y nevoso, la niña de diez años de edad, Gregorio Kathryn estaba construyendo un fuerte de nieve cuado las muñecas les empezó a doler porque estaban frías y húmedas. Ella resolvio el problema y invento "Writies", y se los puso debajo de su abrigo y guantes ".

Kathryn invento y patentado "Wristies". "Wristies" son ropa protectiva de invierno que está diseñada para el usado debajo del abrigo y los guantes para bloquear la nieve, el viento y el frío de entrar en los huecos sin protección.

También, mientras que la inventora, Kathryn Gregory comenzó "Wristies", Inc, una compañía para fabrica y vende "Wristies". La empresaria ha hecho acuerdos con las Girl Scouts, Federal Express, y McDonanlds. En 1997 Kathryn Gregorio se convirtió en la persona más joven en aparecer en QVC, la cadena de televisión comercial.

Tú también puedes sentir "el dolor" de alguna situación incómoda o amenazante y pensar en diseñar algo para disminuir la molestia. Esto podría ser el momento del "descubrimiento" tuyo y a un estilo de vida generoso en lugar de vivir de cheque de pago a cheque de pago. Incluso si tú eres sólo una mesera tal vez podría sugerirle a su jefe que él tenga toallas de banda de 8" x 11" para las meseras y ayudantes de cocina para usar que no sólo son útil para limpiar rápidamente los derrames, sino que tambien tengan bordados "ESPERAMOS QUE REGRESEN!" Phil G. EL PROPIETARIO.

Ve a casa y consegue una toalla de tú mamá y encuentra una empresa de bordados en las páginas amarillas. Cobrarán $8-10 para el bordado. Muestrale a tu jefe. Le puede gustar la idea. Si no, pronto te verá como una persona en lugar de un número y, posiblemente, te promocionara para supervisor.

Los atletas, matemáticos, violinistas, y escritores que lean este libro reconocerán que esto es "estar en la zona". Esto sucede cuando por un momento tu mente está temporalmente inmune a las irritaciones de lo que te rodea. Tu enfoque está tan centrado que la respuesta a tu próxima movida parece tan clara que puedes visualizar los resultados antes de actuar.

Si permites que alguien aprecie la distinción entre IDEAS y CREENCIAS madurarás ganando dinero al descubrir IDEAS y ser un líder dentro de tu ramo. Si estás dispuesto a explorar nuevas IDEAS y rehúsas ser limitado por las CREENCIAS negativas de otros (como "nunca funcionará"), entonces lógicamente las usarás a tu favor en los próximos meses para solucionar tus problemas o ganar más dinero.

El lado negativo es que estas revelaciones se evaporan rápidamente. Tu mente permite que tus CREENCIAS te hagan regresar a tu rutina típica. Sin embargo, al haber actuado, has hecho uno o dos pasos hacia adelante en tu camino a llegar a ser millonario. Si juegas al juego de Monopoly, tus acciones son como haber tomado tu pieza y haber movido uno o dos cuadros hacia el "Boardwalk" o "Park Place".

Cuando menciono IDEAS contra CREENCIAS, trata de apreciar el hecho de que la mayoría de los adultos no pueden captar el significado de este concepto. Esto es algo bastante sofisticado y muchos adultos lo igualan a "tratar de clavar gelatina a la pared". Muchos adultos no quieren tomarse el tiempo para pensar en esto porque seria un desafío a su rutina de creencias rígidas. Yo mismo lo pensé mucho tiempo antes de incluirlo en este libro. Decidí incluirlo porque sus mentes jóvenes están dispuestas a cosas nuevas, lo menos que pude hacer es simplemente hacerles saber que existía el tema, y de esta manera aprenderán a ganar más dinero del que jamás podrían gastar. Muchos de ustedes, por su edad, simplemente repasarán rápidamente este concepto y eso no está mal. Pero quizás existan uno o dos de ustedes a quienes les gustaría aprender un poco mas acerca de estas IDEAS y CREENCIAS, por lo que he incluido mas información detallada en el "Apéndice" de este libro, bajo el título de 'metafísica'. Si te estás preguntando porque he incluido este tema en este libro que se trata sobre ganar dinero, es porque puede ser el la base para todo tu futuro de éxito, tanto en lo personal como en lo material, tal como ha sido para mí.

Las CREENCIAS cambian constantemente, así que no les pongas toda tu confianza. En contraste, las buenas IDEAS nunca cambian, así que siempre puedes confiar en ellas. Recuerda, "Sólo existen buenas IDEAS. Las malas IDEAS sólo son CREENCIAS disfrazadas".

CREENCIAS	IDEAS
Cambian constante mente:	*No cambian nunca:*
Miedo al futuro	*Sabiduría y comprensíon*
Algunos Resultados:	Algunos Resultados:
Parte más baja de la cadena alimentaria	Certidumbre
	Dias alegres
Ningun amigo verdadero	Compañerisimo largo y sincero
Culpa, vergúenza, venganza por odio	Respeto de la familia
Matrimonio poco duradero	
Hijos que no quieren nada que ver contigo	

Diagrama De Apoyo

Creencias v. Ideas

Una vez que hayas entendido la distinción entre IDEAS y CREENCIAS, quizás te sientas confuso por ser "demasiado" para tu limitada experiencia en relación a la verdad, o quizás sientas una calma diferente a los temores e incertidumbres sobre el futuro que muchos sienten hasta morir. Una vez que entiendas lo que te he tratado de brindar, caminarás fuera de la oscuridad de la ignorancia y darás paso a la luz brillante de la verdad. Será similar a la flor que no puede regresar a su estado de semilla. Sólo puedes seguir adelante y desarrollar tu potencial completo. Considera leer los dos párrafos precedentes unas cuantas veces y piensa sobre el tema de las IDEAS contra las CREENCIAS. A mí me tomó varios años llegar a lo poco que entiendo sobre el tema. Sin embargo, si por lo menos empiezas a contemplar el concepto, el resultado final será que podrás separar tus problemas de las IDEAS inmutables, en contraste a las CREENCIAS que siempre cambian. Entender esta diferencia por sí sola probablemente te recompensará. Entonces podrás sin duda disfrutar una experiencia adulta con las personas que te rodean, porque percibirán tu fuerza y la serenidad que muestras bajo presión, y te felicitarán continuamente por la manera como manejas los asuntos.

No es importante que entiendas todo el significado de este Libro en una sola lectura. Sin embargo, empezando ahora, considera meditar sobre el concepto de que las buenas IDEAS son permanentes y nunca cambian, y te darán una sensación de paz y seguridad. Las buenas IDEAS (salud, felicidad, y regocijo) son accesibles a todos y no se ven afectadas por cualquier irritación de las que ocurren día tras día.

Las CREENCIAS y los rituales humanos (temor, culpa, pena, coraje) cambian constantemente. Son conceptos inventados por el hombre que te lastiman al igual que te ayudan, porque te mantienen constantemente agitado y en desequilibrio. Éste es otro tema completamente diferente fuera del alcance de este libro, pero con el hecho de que lo he mencionado, sabrás que este tema existe, y que se lo puede estudiar. Si algún día puedes ayudar a un amigo cuando su vida esté en problemas, entonces he hecho un buen trabajo con simplemente mencionarlo.

Hablemos sobre la Regla 2; "No puedes ayudar a otra persona, sin ayudarte a ti mismo". Estamos hablando del esfuerzo de consuelo que darás de tu parte, no de las cosas físicas. Darle a alguien "la camisa que llevas en tu espalda", cuando es la única camisa que tienes, no es una idea muy sabia. Esforzarte por enseñar a otra persona cómo obtener una camisa nueva, es una mejor idea. Algunos de ustedes ya están familiarizados con lo bueno que se siente tomarse el tiempo para enseñarle algo a un hermano o hermana menor. Te siguen por toda la casa considerándote como la fuente de todo conocimiento. Al día siguiente, después que te hayas tomado el tiempo de llegar a su corazón, te sentirás recompensado. Una vez que te tomes el tiempo con ellos, recibirás el premio de anotar el tanto ganador en ese importantísimo juego de fútbol. Es el mismo sentimiento que sintió una persona mayor al enseñarte algo.

No debes buscar a pobres para darles dinero, ellos repudiarán tus buenas intenciones por haberlos insultado. Es mejor darles ayuda por medio de tu tiempo, paciencia, y tu comprensión para enseñarles a salir de la pobreza. Si te critican porque no les ofreciste dinero, obviamente no quieren salir de la pobreza. Simplemente quieren gastar tu dinero en las cosas donde actualmente están desperdiciando el suyo, como juegos de azar, alcohol, drogas, etc. De nuevo: no vayas más allá de lo que es tu obligación, posiblemente solo tú notarás esto. Sin embargo te sentirás bien contigo mismo, encontrarás una manera de premiarte y estarás un poco más cerca de ser millonario.

Pon tus pensamientos en escrito

Padres

Para bien o para mal, todos al crecer teníamos alguien más con quien lidiar. Para los que siempre tenían a sus padres accesibles cuando los necesitaban, no simplemente cuando tenían ganas de ayudarte: trata de visualizar ese acto de caridad que te demostraron. Si fuiste bendecido con ojos que ven y oídos que oyen, seria bueno considerar el decirle a tus padres que reconoces y agradeces sus sacrificios.

Les darás satisfacción con sólo reconocer sus esfuerzos por tolerar tu joven y siempre cambiante punto de vista. Sin salirme del tema de este libro, tus padres, a su vez, se sentirán bien consigo mismos, lo que los ayudará a tomar buenas decisiones en sus ramos respectivos y posiblemente acaben asegurándose un mejor futuro financiero, todo a causa de tus pocas palabras. Tus palabras cálidas son como una recompensa a tus padres y hasta es posible que los emociones hasta las lágrimas.

Con los años, cuando tengas tus propios hijos, recuérdate la importancia de ser accesible cuando te necesiten, recuerda que tú alguna vez estuviste en la misma situación, y no lo hagas sólo por la convivencia. Es probable que tus hijos, a su vez, sean considerados y sinceros contigo y aprecien lo que tú haces por ellos.

Algunas veces, un joven se desvía y un padre tiene que decidir darle apoyo o no a un joven de 17 años, echado a perder, egoísta, mal hablado y malcriado, pero tú te darás cuenta de ello cuando te toque.

El punto es que cuando como padre tú estas presente con tus hijos, hasta tú mismo te sentirás bien como padre, y tú también te premiarás en el mercado de la vida. Este se repiterá de ciclo en ciclo.

Considera preguntarle a tu mamá o papá o a un familiar exitoso si es mejor trabajar para alguien por el resto de tu vida o si es mejor empezar un negocio y trabajar por uno mismo en la primera oportunidad que se presenta. A tu edad, es un poco abrumador pensar sobre manejar tu propio negocio. El complejo compromiso de pagar salarios, renta, mantener un inventario, pagar impuestos, etc., es demasiado para guardar en tu mente durante los próximos años. Por lo pronto, disfruta los altibajos con tus amigos y todo te saldrá bien si empiezas a ahorrar dinero desde ahora.

Empezar hoy

A tu edad de estudiante, ¿cómo empiezas a ahorrar si no tienes dinero aparte de unos dólares que ganas de algún trabajito de media jornada o dinero que recibiste de tu abuela en tu cumpleaños? Debes hacer lo que todo millonario ha hecho cuando todavía no desarrollaban un talento a tu edad. Abre una cuenta bancaria. Entonces enfócate en acumular dinero tal como hicieras con una colección de tarjetas de béisbol, lápices de labios, estampillas de correo, o artículos de revistas de tu estrella de cine. Busca trabajo para que cada mes que pase acumules más ahorros en tu cuenta bancaria, y cada mes que pasa trata de acumular más que el mes pasado. Es como un juego de acumular lo más que puedas sin mencionárselo nadie. Es como levantar pesas o hacer repeticiones de ejercicios o sacar buenas notas en la escuela: hazlo simplemente para comprobarte a ti mismo que lo puedes lograr. Muchas veces vemos esto en las películas donde el joven actor o actriz se esmera por destacarse en un deporte para probar que puede lograrlo. No lo hacen sólo por recibir la admiración del auditorio, sino más bien para conseguir la conquista o el respeto de uno mismo, especialmente si tú eres el auditorio que se da cuenta de tus logros.

¿Y qué hay en cuanto a gastar dinero en tus actividades favoritas? Cada persona debe decidir sus prioridades sobre la forma de gastar su propio dinero de regalos de cumpleaños, etc. Aunque tengas que usar todos tus ahorros para una emergencia familiar, ten la seguridad de que siempre puedes empezar de nuevo. La emergencia que surja solo demorará tu camino a ser millonario. En lo relativo a cosas diarias, deja que tus amigas despilfarren su dinero en coches, DVDs, joyas, cambiar del color de su pelo, etc. Tú sigue ahorrando dinero en el banco.

Considera no tener un auto y usar una bicicleta como transporte. Con los precios actuales te costará como mínimo unos $300 por mes financiar un auto nuevo. Haz todo lo posible por no endeudarte con nadie (con excepción de una hipoteca de casa en unos años). Si quieres transporte confiable cada vez que la necesites, considera pagarle a un amigo $20 de gasolina cuando salgan a una doble cita. Es mejor que gastar los $16 que gasta tu amigo por sí solo cada vez que maneja unas 20 millas para una cita. Esos $16 incluyen la gasolina, el aceite del coche, reparaciones, seguro de auto, y los cobros de la financiera que tiene el carro. Pagándole a tu amigo más dinero que lo que consumirá en una cita, estará muy dispuesto a darte un aventón a cualquier lugar que quieras llegar, porque estarías cubriendo los gastos inmediatos que el o ella tengan. Un taxi te costaría $30 por las mismas 20 millas. Así constantemente saldrás adelante, evitarás las irritaciones de ser dueño de un carro con todos los gastos, y tendrás una reputación alrededor de tu escuela por ser una persona generosa.

En cualquier caso, nunca te quedes corto en lo que le das a tu amigo para el aventón. Quizás razones que no le cuesta mucho más llevarte como pasajero y entonces desees no pagarle nada. Ese tipo de razonamiento infantil tendrá malos resultados y perderás a tu amigo.

Actualmente (2011), cuesta entre 75 a 80 centavos por milla mantener un auto (cambiando cada dia). El dinero que tu amigo haya ahorrado ya desapareció, mientras su auto se deteriora al punto de no servir. Cuando alguien pide prestado dinero para una inversión que se deteriora, como un coche, nunca hay suficiente dinero para los ahorros. Nunca podrás desarrollar tu carrera para ser millonario si estás siempre corto de dinero. A menos que el auto que compres gane dinero: por ejemplo, un taxista puede justificar el gasto de un auto y a la misma vez usarlo para su transporte personal. Ese ángulo le permite pagar su coche y hasta quedarse con lo que sobra. Muchos conductores de taxi empezaron con un solo auto financiado y al trabajar 12 horas, siete días a las semana, tras unos 5 años acabaron siendo dueños de 20 taxis con 20 empleados. Durante esos 5 años iniciales, ese taxista se benefició de usar el taxi para transporte personal sin costarle casi nada. Era una situación ideal para él.

Así, sería bueno que mientras leas este libro decidas qué tiene más importancia. Cuando llegues a los 35 años de edad, ¿será mejor volar en primera clase a Cancún, México, por un fin de semana, sólo porque te da la gana?. ¿O será mejor vivir en un apartamento rentado junto con la visita ocasional al cine local o a la cantina de la semana? No puedes tenerlo de las dos maneras.

Si eres débil, escogerás despilfarrar tu dinero en vez de ahorrarlo y votarás por el político que promete incrementar la ayuda pública porque estás a punto de perder tu trabajo: ése es el resultado de no ahorrar dinero. Si ahorras dinero, tienes un sentido de haber cumplido contigo mismo y tendrás más autodominio sobre otras cosas que conlleva este mundo. Entonces llegarás a ser tú mismo en el sentido material. Mantén en mente que ser tú mismo muchas veces conlleva más satisfacción que el dinero mismo en muchos casos, pero este es un tema fuera de los límites de este libro.

Que afortunado eres

Mírate en el espejo ahora mismo. Nota tu sonrisa, la claridad de tus ojos, y tus expresiones faciales. Ahora, cuando tengas la oportunidad, fíjate en algunos de tus compañeros de clase. Toma nota de los tímidos que solo quieren estar a solas. Quizás ellos ya "se dieron por vencidos" porque les afectó algo negativo en sus vidas cuando eran más jóvenes. Hasta que un maestro o compañero de clase logra motivarlos, de lo contrario seguirán su camino con el semblante caído porque sienten que el futuro no les depara nada bueno. Fíjate en tus compañeros de clase que se pintan el pelo o se colocan aretes en la piel. Su necesidad es impresionar al mundo con oro y plata, decir qué tan diferentes son o que están a la moda o lo hacen motivados por la diversión, o quizás sus acciones son un desafío a sus padres que siempre andan encima de ellos.

Digo esto no para insultar a quienes tienen costumbres étnicas o religiosas que los obligan a adornarse la piel para distinguir sus orígenes religiosos, familiares o geográficos. Esas razones tienen su motivos legítimos. Sin embargo, si la meta de adornarse la piel es una muestra de rebelión y ese estudiante está deprimido por un hecho de su vida personal, entonces las ideas que se encuentran en este libro son prematuras para ese individuo. Quizás puedas ayudar a alguien en este estado simplemente dándole buenas palabras y asegurándole que no es anormal. Quizás algunos aprecien tus buenas palabras en vez de rechazarte. Quizás algunos de ellos lleguen a enderezarse por causa de que "tú ayudaste a alguien". Con este pequeño acto de caridad de tu parte, tal como una sonrisa o un acto de ayuda, tú te sentirás bien y actuarás para tu beneficio y lograrás hacer una diferencia en tu futuro financiero.

Un ejemplo – comprobando mis sugerencias – sería en el próximo baile de tu escuela (si ese tipo de cosa siquiera existe todavía). Considera sacar a bailar a un muchacho o muchacha con quien nunca hayas bailado. Fíjate en los ojos de esa persona. Quizás le dé tanta alegría ser escogido o escogida que se tropezarán en el baile por tanto júbilo. Observa cuán bien te sentirás contigo mismo al final del baile. Tu satisfacción interna o júbilo que acompaña tal acto de caridad te dará un indicio de la razón por la cual yo mismo me he tomado el tiempo para escribir este libro.

Enséñame el Dinero

Digamos que muchos de ustedes tienen en su cuenta bancaria unos $300 a $500 procedentes de algún. La sugerencia normal que te dará un padre o un tutor es que no toques tu dinero y lo dejes en tu cuenta bancaria para ganarte un pequeño interés. Esto puede ser una buena idea cuando seas mayor y tengas las obligaciones de una familia. No es necesariamente lo ideal para un adolescente que quiere empezar su carrera de millonario.

Algunos amigos o tu familia te dirán que $500 es muy poco para comprar acciones en el mercado mercantil o cualquier otra inversión. Todos tenemos que trabajar con lo que tenemos y actuar de acuerdo a nuestras fuerzas. Una ganancia de 200% con nuestros $500,00 es igual que una ganancia de 200% sobre $100.000. Lo importante es cuán listo estás "en la caza" (comprando y vendiendo). El volumen de carne (ganancia) con el que regresas a casa es cosa secundaria.

Si es posible, empieza esta semana, mientras todavía tengas esto fresco en la mente. Si te detienes, posiblemente pase el año y sigas sólo hablando sobre mis sugerencias; así habrás perdido muchas oportunidades. Tienes toda tu vida por delante, busca consejos de un adulto que respetas sobre lo visto en este libro, quien tome tus ahorros y los invierta por ti de la forma que te guste. No debes ser tonto y tirar tu dinero en las carreras o el casino; será mejor que hables con alguna persona de negocios que te parezca exitosa y le preguntes como puedes tomar $500 y convertirlo en $1500 en tres años.

Tú "sobrevives" trabajando 12 horas al día.
Te "haces rico" haciendo que tu dinero
gane dinero por ti.

Ahora que la inflación empieza a subir la cabeza, quizás quieras considerar doblar o triplicar tus cuentas bancarias o comprar monedas de oro. Inflación es un término o concepto que mucha gente no entiende ni aprecia. En lo que concierne a tus ahorros, es como comparar tu trabajo de media jornada al pago que tú recibirás en unos tres años. El lado bueno es que ahora tú recibes unos $8,00 por hora, pero en unos tres años el mismo trabajo pagará $20,00 por hora. Lo que tiene de malo es que un boleto de película te costará $25,00 o un par de pantalones de mezclilla te costará unos $330,00 en vez de los precios que pagas actualmente. Si tu dinero se queda en una cuenta bancaria, pierde su poder de compra cada año.

Considera buscar las direcciones de las tiendas donde vendan monedas en tu localidad, y cuando llegues ahí busca al dueño de la tienda para que te eduque sobre cómo puedes proteger tus $500 mientras a la vez ganas el doble o el triple de tu dinero en los próximos años. Considera que un adulto te enseñe a abrir una cuenta de acciones con un corredor de bolsa. Observa las acciones de oro o plata en línea con el dólar más alto. Personalmente, estoy interesado en las acciones de una compañía que busca oro y plata. En el 2001 esta compañía encontró el depósito más grande de oro en Alaska y el segundo depósito de cobre más grande que el mundo haya visto a unas 16 millas del pueblo de Iliamna, Alaska, cerca de la bahía de Bristol. Búscalo en un mapa, los detalles se encuentran en la sección de referencias. También he añadido en la sección de referencia otros dos ejemplos de acciones comunes, que yo pienso se incrementarán en un 300%-400% en unos años, no como recomendaciones, sino para que las vigiles, sencillamente para saber si yo estaba equivocado.

Igual que en las películas de vaqueros

Lo siguiente es un ejemplo de hasta donde puede llevarte tu imaginación sin barreras. Si las compañías mencionadas anteriormente reciben el permiso necesario del estado de Alaska para extraer los metales preciosos y logran sobrellevar los obstáculos del ambiente, en solo cinco años, estas compañías gastarán unos $ 3.000 millones de dólares para maquinaria, para abrir la mina y para construir una carretera desde la mina al puerto marítimo. También necesitarán 2.000 mineros y administradores. Necesitarán casas y tiendas para un pueblo ubicado en un área remota.

Si llegas a ser dueño de sus acciones, y solicitas un empleo en las oficinas de esa empresa en Vancouver, Canadá, puedes mencionar donde te enteraste de esto. Así te asegurarás llegar lejos con esa profesión. Quizás hasta te guste ser un precursor en lo desconocido, lo que requerirá que uses pistola cuando salgas del campamento o cuando viajes al río. El lado malo es que tendrás por vecinos a osos y leones y la nieve alcanza los ocho pies de altura en el invierno. El lado agradable es que tendrás una aventura que recordarás toda tu vida. Lograrás lo que hombres y mujeres sólo anhelan en plática. Con 2000 nuevos residentes habrá un sinfín de oportunidades. Tú puedes ser agente inmobiliario, constructor de casas, dueño de un restaurante o una tienda, abrir un centro de atención de niños y mucho más, antes de llegar a tener 26 años de edad. Al hacer cualquiera de estas cosas. puedes recibir una atractiva ganancia trabajando en esto sólo por las tardes o durante los fines de semana. Si comparas con quedarte en el mismo pueblo donde te criaste, sin obtener logros financieros, podrás ahorrar mucho en el banco local de Alaska, ¡Porque en Alaska se paga más y no tienes mucho en que gastarlo! (La razón porque se paga más es porque es un sacrificio el estar en un ambiente sin las comodidades y servicios urbanos.) Llévate muchos libros para leer y una lámpara porque no habrá mucho más que hacer al atardecer. Quizás en tu tiempo libre te pongas a buscar oro por tu cuenta para suplementar tu ingreso.

Una vez que hayas invertido un poco de años en Alaska, tendrás suficiente ahorros, o si a esta altura tus acciones han incrementado bastante su valor, puedes venderlas y dejar tu trabajo. Ahora puedes tomar tu dinero y hacer tu primera inversión en un terreno, un avión, una excursión de pesca o cacería, o una tienda de joyas en tu pueblo natal, o lo que te parezca bien: has ahorrado una buena porción de tus ganancias o regalos.

Capítulo Tres
"LAS COSAS PRÁCTICAS"

"Nunca es demasiado tarde para llegar a ser lo que pudieras haber sido. Esto gratificará a algunos y asombrará a los demás."
– Anónimo

Tu primer trabajo de tiempo completo

Si la idea de Alaska no te parece bien, dejémosla de lado y establece cómo puedes ganar dinero cuando ya no tengas el cuidado de mamá y papá. Lo más difícil es encontrar un trabajo al salir de la preparatoria o del colegio. Algunas escuelas tienen "eventos de carreras". Allí estarán adultos dando detalles de cómo se ganan la vida – tienen buenas intenciones pero frecuentemente estos eventos son aburridos. Si el orador simplemente preguntara qué quiere escuchar el estudiante, entonces se sacaría más provecho.

En esos días de carrera, cuando yo me presento frente a estudiantes, les hago preguntas sobre qué hechos recientes han ocurrido en la escuela y tienen presente antes de que yo empiece mi discurso. Si no logro esto, estoy perdiendo mi tiempo y el de ellos al describir mi carrera. ¿A quién le importa lo que yo hago en mi carrera? Sólo les importa lo que tienen en mente en ese momento. Si ellos me comentan que cosas les son de importancia, tenemos algo en que basar nuestra plática. Como no tengo el lujo de escuchar tus puntos de vista, aquí hay otro intento que quizás te parezca adecuado sobre el tema de tu primer trabajo. Desde luego, necesitas un trabajo antes de ser millonario, principalmente para adquirir la experiencia, por eso es apropiado que recibas sugerencias sobre cómo obtener un buen trabajo.

Ropa

Tocaremos algunos puntos importantes que te ayudarán a ganarte el respeto de la persona que te está entrevistando. La cosa más importante a considerar es la ropa que vistes. Desde luego, la persona que te entrevista no te conoce, así que se guiará por "las primeras apariencias".

Tienes que esmerarte en cómo vestirte para esa entrevista. Es como cuando llega un estudiante nuevo a tu escuela, te formas una opinión de él o ella al ver como se viste, si es un ganador o un ñoño. Ten en mente que toda sociedad tiene su código de vestimenta, desde el uso de colores vivos al uso de tatuajes para decorar el cuerpo, o ponerse trajes de tres piezas, una camisa formal con su corbata roja, etc. Estas sólo son una creencias, pero si no te vistes según el código de la tribu, no serás aceptado.

Piensa de tu ropa como un disfraz. Imagina que la oficina donde serás entrevistado es el teatro. El que te entrevista es tu audiencia y tú eres el actor. Si entras usando una camiseta de colores escandalosos o tenis de gimnasia mientras todos los demás empleados entran con una camisa blanca y zapatos brillosos, no llegaras ni cercas a obtener ese trabajo. La razón es la misma por la cual un equipo de fútbol usa el mismo uniforme. Significa que tú, como miembro del equipo, estás dispuesto a vestirte y trabajar bajo las mismas reglas del juego. Fíjate en tu clase o lugar de almuerzo. Todos los que se juntan en grupitos se visten igual, casi como un disfraz, el mismo estilo de pelo y maquillaje. Si alguien dentro de ese grupo decide vestirse de otro disfraz, probablemente se sentarían junto a los de otra tribu, donde los aceptarían tal como son.

Para darte cuenta cómo debes vestirte para una entrevista, investiga un poco antes de llamar a la empresa que visitarás.

Considera ser franco y preguntar a la recepcionista, "¿me puede decir cómo se viste el gerente de cierto departamento? "Estoy considerando un trabajo e esta empresa y quiero llegar vestido apropiadamente." Si eso no funciona, pregúntale a una persona mayor, a quien tú respetes, y pregúntale qué recomendaría.

Asumamos que es un trabajo de oficina que requiere camisa blanca, zapatos de vestir, pantalones planchados y un cinturón formal, de manera que tus pantalones no cuelguen. Si es necesario, pide prestada la ropa de tu hermano o hermana mayor. ¿Qué piensas ahora? Muchos de ustedes se avergonzarían Considera hablar con la persona que te entrevistó y pregúntale que resaltó de la persona a quien se le dio el empleo. También pregúntale cómo podrías haber llegado más preparado a la entrevista. Al despedirte menciona que te gustaría ser considerado una segunda vez si la persona que ganó el puesto no cumple, o si llega a existir otra posición.

A la persona que te entrevista seguramente le sorprenderá que a tu edad hables con tanta franqueza y confianza de ti mismo. Esa persona te considerará más que un simple "muchacho o muchacha buscando un trabajo" y habrá una fuerte posibilidad que la persona te recuerde entre otros. Todo empleador quiere conseguir a alguien que sobresalga. Hasta quizás a ti te guste rodearte de amigos que se defienden o sean aventureros. No te juntarías con personas tímidas o depresivas, entonces no tejes deprimir sólo porque tu primera entrevista no fue exitosa. En las películas, nos gusta ver que el chico no se dé por vencido y que se levante contra lo establecido. A las empresas les gusta incorporar individuos como estos porque ganan mucho dinero para ellas. Los tímidos o temerosos se quedan callados al ser criticados y no tienen la confianza para levantar la voz y sugerir cambios o mejoras en su lugar de trabajo.

Platiquemos un poco en cuanto a tu ropa. Tú escogiste el disfraz que tienes puesto ahora mismo posiblemente porque tus amigos se visten de la misma manera. Quizás debas quedarte con esa ropa cuando estés con ellos, pero para influenciar a clientes o extraños para que te paguen dinero, debes impresionarlos favorablemente para que logres su confianza. En general, las personas más bien vestidas son las más respetados. Todos nos intimidamos un poco si pasan y nuestro vestir es un poco casual. Si te ves el programa de los Oscars cada año puedes ver ejemplos de el publico bajando la cabeza cada vez que una mujer bien vestida camina.

Quizás sintamos un poco de envidia o coraje porque no te vistes tan bien, pero todavía respetamos su autoridad por la manera en que están disfrazados. Esto los llevará a pensar sobre un disfraz que los haga parecer exitosos. El beneficio de este "disfraz" es que otras personas asumirán que eres intelectual, o quizás rico. Esto significará que la persona entrevistándote te tomará como un candidato más serio en vez de un joven sin experiencia, del cual se quiere deshacer rápidamente.

El que te entrevista sabe cómo se viste el jefe diariamente. Si tú te vistes como el jefe, existe una relación mental: tú y el patrón son de la misma tribu. Él o ella deben tener cuidado en no ofenderte. Quizás a la persona que te entreviste le convenga darte el trabajo simplemente por su conveniencia, para que el jefe note que te vistes como él. Quizás hasta el jefe elogie al que te entrevistó, al mencionarle que parece que "encajarás" fácilmente en la empresa. Esto se traduce en un posible aumento de sueldo para la persona que te entrevistó.

En la sección de referencias en este libro yo menciono un libro titulado "Dress For Success" ("Vestirse para el éxito"). Lo utilicé como guía en mis inicios, y tú deberías considerar conseguir una copia y estudiarlo con el mismo entusiasmo como si fuera la última edición de la revista People. Si no puedes encontrar una edición nueva, busca en la Internet un libro usado a mitad de precio.

CÓMO NO CONSEGUIR EL EMPLEO

La persona que te entrevista probablemente sea una persona buena, de familia, con hijos en tu edad. Emplearán a muchachos y muchachas de tu edad y desearán que sus hijos lleguen a comportarse o vestirse como ellos. Si vienes a la entrevista vestido de forma 'extrema', estarás batallando por no durar siquiera un rato en la entrevista.

Mencionaré algunos errores graves que muchos jóvenes cometen porque nadie les avisó de antemano sobre lo que ofendería al que te entrevista:

- El masticarse la uñas excesivamente (Si es un hábito de nerviosismo y no te da suficiente tiempo para crecer las uñas, entonces explícale que estás intentando poner fin a ese hábito. Esto demostrará que estás alerta al problema y que tienes valor.)

- Pinturas de uña no apropiadas como negro, verde, azul, etc.

- Uñas sucias

- Cualquier ornamento inexplicable en la piel como un tatuaje o arete

- Cualquier olor fuerte ya sea perfume, colonia o de higiene personal

- Zapatos que no estén limpios.

- Pantalones que cuelguen

- Cualquier insinuación sensual como mostrar mucho el busto, el ombligo, o pantalones ajustados
- Pinturas de pelo no naturales como tiras de azul, morado, o partes brillosas
- Pelo cortado de una manera 'extrema' o con un estilo 'extremo'.
- Ropa que no le queda a la persona, rasgada, sucia, o mal planchada.

Tendrás que juzgarlo por ti mismo, pero seria bueno asegurarse de tu apariencia antes de ir a la entrevista, solicitando la opinión de algún adulto.

Sobre el tema de ustedes que buscan su primer trabajo oficial, me encontré un artículo de entretenimiento en el Reader 's Digest (Septiembre 2009 Página Número 110) que tiene que ver con las hojas de vida. Parecía apropiado para los adolescentes para que eviten errores clásicos. Burlense y luego recuerden quando llenen su hoja de vida. Mira si reconoces la ironía de los autores que siguen:

Historial de empleo:

Ultimo trabajo – "Supervisor de restaurante. Limpiaba y supervisaba empleados."

Trabajo antes de ese – "CFO de una tienda de pantalones de mujeres. Tambien teniamos de hombres."

Trabajo antes de ese – "Pobre tipo. Abandonava mis pertenencias y estilo de vida."

Referencias:

"Mi amigo Scott"
"Mi novia"
"Ninguno, yo he dejado un camino de destrucción."

Intereses:
"Chismes"
"Sexo"

Habilidades:
"Fluido en el Spanol y el Ingles."
"Buena memoria, aptitud sólida de matemáticas, buena memoria."
"Puedo escribir sinmirar el tecladoo"
"Capaz de silbar mientras pretender beber agua, al mismo tiempo."

Educación:
"Universidad de Morón"
"Asisti a cursos de la univarsidad."

Logros académicos:
"Recibió la beca Smith por su excelencia en Inglish."
En general, si te vistes limpiamente y nítidamente, todo saldrá bien. En esencia, tu apariencia emite tu deseo de aceptar la autoridad o recibir órdenes en una estructura empresarial. Ésta es una manera sobre cómo demostrarle al mundo que no serás un malcriado al momento de ser empleado.

Pagar por tu disfraz

Ahora bien, ¿cómo puede alguien que no tiene mucho dinero comprarse buena ropa cara? La respuesta es "No Lo Hagas". Busca una tienda de reventa en tu localidad por medio del directorio telefónico o Internet. Estará a cargo de algún hospital o alguna iglesia. Ellos recolectarán ropa de alta calidad de personas ricas que utiliza la ropa pocas veces y luego las donan para recibir un recorte en los impuestos o porque han engordado o simplemente ya no les gusta el estilo. Estas tiendas de reventa suelen vender un traje de $1000 que sólo se ha usado unas 10 veces a sólo $20. Hasta las mandan a la tintorería antes de ponerlas a la venta. El millonario que donó su ropa dedujo unos $200 de su impuestos – él también sale ganando. Cuando seas mayor podrás comprar ropa de alta calidad a precio completo. Pero por ahora no tiene sentido comprar ropa cara cuando todavía estás en desarrollo.

Cuando tengas unos 25 años podrás ordenarte un traje hecho a mano en Oriente a la mitad del precio de los que se hacen aquí en los Estados Unidos. Sencillamente busca bajo Sastres en Internet o las páginas amarillas.

En la sección de referencias he puesto el teléfono de un sastre que viaja a todas las ciudades metropolitanas por todo los EUA a base mensual para medir a sus clientes. Nos conocimos al principio de la década de 1960 cuando él apenas había llegado de la India, y ha sido sastre de toda mi familia desde entonces.

Capítulo Cuatro
"Tus elecciones Personales"

"La Regla de Oro – El que tiene el oro manda"

Dar órdenes o recibir órdenes
La idea principal que me gustaría fijar en tu memoria es la siguiente...

¡MUY POCAS PERSONAS LOGRAN SER RICOS TRABAJANDO PARA OTRA PERSONA!

(Sin embargo, al principio es posible que sea necesario, para aprender las particularidades de algún negocio o para conocer las reglas necesarias para el éxito)

Hasta ahora la herramienta más poderosa para que puedas tomar control de tu futuro está y ha estado siempre completamente bajo tu dominio, y es tu habilidad de auto distenderte. Éste es el verdadero factor que determinará cuán exitoso serás en todo aspecto de tu vida. Cuando entres a tu penúltimo y último año de la preparatoria considera la lógica por la cual no has podido ahorrar dinero si fumas, consumes drogas, o si tomas más de una cerveza o dos por semana. No estoy juzgando tus preferencias personales. Sin embargo, si insistes en gastar dinero en cosas que desaparecerán en unos instantes (gastar $200 en cohetes para el 4 de Julio es dejar literalmente que tu ahorros se hagan humo), arrastrarás contigo un gran peso en tu camino al éxito financiero.

¿Has pensado siquiera el costo semanal de usar tabaco, drogas o alcohol? Te aseguro que el costo excede $50.00

por semana. En ese caso, estamos hablando de $2,000-$3,000 por año. Si hubieras invertido $1,000 de ese dinero en vez de gastarlo, se te habría triplicado en 3-5 años, podrías establecer cimientos sobre los cuales podrías edificar tu imperio. Todo el concepto es más fácil de decir que de hacer. Todavía puedes salir y disfrutar de muchas cosas para experimentar la vida a tu alrededor, pero considera simplemente empezar a usar tu capacidad mental para disciplinarte.

He aquí un reto que puedes intentar lograr en una o dos semanas. Trata de depositar en una caja sobre el tocador el equivalente a lo que gastas en cigarrillos o cualquier hábito que tengas, todos los días. Te sorprenderás cuánto puedes ahorrar. No solamente te beneficiaras económicamente, sino también alcanzaras un alto "dominio" sobre ti mismo por haberlo logrado. Tendrás la auto-satisfacción en saber que no existe ningún reto económico que no puedas conquistar. Cuando veas cuán fuerte eres en el arte de la auto-disciplina, lograr una fortuna en dinero será cosa del diario.

Aunque no te interese mucho la carrera para ser rico, después de haber leído este libro tendrás el dinero suficiente cuando llegue el momento de comprarte tu primer auto o motocicleta. Una joven de 19 años, recién graduada, me contó que pudo comprarse un par de botas, ropa de marca y viajar a la Florida en sus vacaciones con el dinero que ahorró durante sus últimos dos años escolares. La joven no está interesada en ser millonaria por sus inversiones (prefiere casarse con "un hombre rico") pero se ha ganado el derecho de gastar su dinero por haber tenido primero la disciplina de ahorrarlo.

Muchos de ustedes quizás consideren que la preparatoria es aburrida, pero si mantienes en mente que eres una persona que vale la pena, y continúas dándote metas, nunca estarás aburrido. Siempre estarás esmerándote por mejorarte a ti mismo. Esto es lo que estoy tratando de impartirte; si tienes confianza en ti mismo, podrás vencer cualquier reto. Podrás sobresalir en cualquier aspecto de tu vida, inclusive ser rico. Los que puedan disciplinarse acabarán con más dinero del necesario. Tu futura pareja se quedará contigo lo suficiente para celebrar tu aniversario 50, porque habrás evitado un divorcio al no tener que pelear por la falta de dinero. Tus hijos te respetarán porque ellos verán el mismo respeto que te tienes a ti mismo. Tus hijos no te harán pasar momentos difíciles como algunos lo hacen con sus padres hoy en día: esto es porque no tienen respeto a los hábitos de sus padres.

Mantén en la mente que la razón por la que tienes dificultad en disciplinarte es porque tus mismos padres no pueden auto-disciplinarse. Todos nosotros queremos ser "como nuestro padre" o "como nuestra madre". Ellos son nuestros modelos. Si tu ambiente en casa está lleno de inseguridades: mucha gritería, humo y latas vacías de cerveza tirada por toda la casa – entonces quizás tu crees el mismo ambiente en tu propia casa.

Por el otro lado, si mamá y papá son adultos centrados y tú eres el malcriado que tiene la boca grande en tu familia, el que es egoísta y desorganizado, entonces considera lo siguiente:

- No hay nada que temer si estás educado para ser organizado y eficiente.

- Seguirás rehusándote a seguir las normas de una sociedad organizada y acabarás siendo un adulto en el último lugar de la cadena alimenticia.

Ésta es una cuestión seria y tendrás que tomar una

decisión ahora; de lo contrario siempre recibirás órdenes de otra persona, porque nunca ahorraste dinero. No tendrás opción. **Visualiza cuán frustrante sería un futuro donde siempre se te "mandará que hacer", todo el tiempo.** Usa esto como fuerza para acumular conocimiento o dinero. Aunque no te interese ser millonario, considera ser el más sabio en el ramo que hayas escogido y tú podrás ser quien da órdenes en vez de no tener más opción que recibir órdenes de tus superiores.

Sé tú mismo

Si ahora vives en un ambiente poco cordial en tu casa, considera no seguir en los pasos de tus padres cuando dejes la casa después de la preparatoria. Debes entender que tienes el derecho a hacerte un adulto en paz. Tú no puedes ser responsable por los hábitos inaceptables que hayan tenido en tu casa. Mamá y papá todavía te amarán porque habrás llegado a ser alguien más exitoso de lo que jamás se podrían imaginar. Aunque traten de desanimarte por lograr más que ellos, tienes que tener suficiente fuerza y valor para ignorar su crítica y llevar adelante tu vida como tú piensas que la debes llevar.

Todos nosotros tenemos una especie de grabadora en nuestras mentes desde el día en que nacimos. Cualquier cosa que se nos haya grabado, ya sea mamá y papá o algún otro recuerdo feliz o deprimente, estará presente en esa grabación desde nuestra más tierna infancia y esto dirige nuestra vida, porque es todo lo que conocemos. Ninguno de nosotros cambia al 100 %, pero todos nosotros podemos modificar nuestro punto de vista y tener un vida adulta gratificante cuanta más educación recibamos.

No tiene sentido usar nuestro ambiente familiar como una excusa por la cual fracasemos económicamente. Trata de comprender que el único tiempo que tiene verdadera importancia son los próximos 5 minutos y cómo usarás el resto del día. Lo que sucedió en la mañana o ayer ya pasó. No puede cambiarse.

Está en tus manos mirarte al espejo y darte permiso para llegar a ser lo que quieras llegar a ser. Si tienes antecedentes negativos en casa, la única manera de parar esa grabadora en tu cabeza es mirarte el espejo y decir a la sociedad: "no puedes evitar que me desarrolle a mi potencial completo". Si no tienes suficiente valor y eres tímido para enfrentarte al espejo, probablemente pasarás la vida viviendo de cheque a cheque, con algún éxito pequeño en tu trabajo. Si tienes algún hermano o hermana menor que te interese, probablemente quieras animarlos a ser "todo lo que puedan ser". ¿Pero por qué tú no haces lo mismo?

Perdónate

Es importante no sentir remordimiento por el pasado. Afortunadamente, ustedes son demasiado jóvenes para sentirse abrumados por la culpabilidad de haber causado daño a otras personas. Al pasar algunos años, alguno de ustedes conducirá un auto alcoholizado, estrellará el coche y causará daño o matará a un pasajero, a ti mismo o a algún niño de 10 años de edad que vaya en su bicicleta. Algunos de ustedes dirán o cometerán alguna tontería con alguna persona con la cual no se debe jugar. Algunos de ustedes pensarán que son muy listos y tratarán de traficar drogas o alguna otra cosa ilegal que lamentarán el resto de sus vidas. Afortunadamente, la gran mayoría de ustedes nunca tendrán que lidiar con estos asuntos indeseables, por la manera en que sus padres los han criado, o porque nacieron con la aptitud de distinguir lo bueno y lo malo.

No estoy aquí para darles un sermón sobre moral, o sobre el daño premeditado que le ocasionarán al prójimo. Eventualmente, los tribunales judiciales se encargarán del daño que ocasionen a otra persona. Lo que me concierne son los accidentes que cometemos diariamente sin intención o la negligencia que podíamos haber evitado. Les quiero dar una fórmula sobre cómo manejar una situación, ya que todos hemos experimentado algún evento no deseable que no podemos cambiar.

Errores... Cuando suceden, tenemos la opción de sumirnos en la depresión, vagar en el estupor hasta que el impacto se quite, o puedes perdonarte al instante. No puedes cambiar lo que sucedió hace 30 segundos ni lo que sucedió ayer. Sin embargo, puedes perdonarte sobre la base de que no cometiste el error intencionalmente. Claro, uno necesita asumir la responsabilidad por haber cometido una falta o pedir perdón, o compensar la falta. Si quieres revolcarte en la pena y la culpa también está bien. Lo que no puedes hacer, si quieres llegar a ser millonario es castigarte a ti mismo y tratar de lavar todos tus errores. Mutilar tu cuerpo no repara el cuerpo de tu víctima. Quédate tranquilo y haz todo lo posible para disminuir el dolor de la persona a la cual dañaste accidentalmente.

Uno se hace daño cuando permanentemente siente culpa y busca formas de castigarse a sí mismo por decir y hacer las cosas equivocadas todos los días. Se necesita ser una persona muy fuerte para perdonarse a uno mismo. No estoy hablando de simplemente ignorar el evento desagradable y convencerse de que nunca sucedió. Tienes que afrontar la verdad y buscar el perdón de la otra persona a quien causaste daño, pero teniendo en mente que no puedes cambiar lo que sucedió ayer. Tienes que tomar lo que queda y avanzar lo mejor que puedas. Debes evitar ser una de esas personas que acaban en un asilo porque insisten en cambiar lo que pasó ayer. Como no pueden revertir lo feo que ha sucedido, repiten la escena en sus mentes una y otra vez; a causa de la culpa y la desilusión que sienten, se ponen contra sí mismos y se aíslan silenciosamente a su propio mundo.

El otro lado de la moneda es perdonar a la persona que te ha causado daño. Esto es muy difícil de hacer. Mientras no puedas perdonarte a ti mismo y perdonar al que te haya ofendido, no podrás avanzar. Caminar arrastrando el peso de no haber perdonado, es demasiado peso para que uno pueda escalarla montaña que implica llegar a ser millonario.

Fíjate en tu propia familia, mira la constante miseria que siente alguien porque todavía siguen sacando a luz el insulto o negligencia en relación a un suceso que tuvo lugar hace muchos años. Considera hablar con esta persona sobre la sugerencia que te he mencionado en relación a perdonar, ya sea a otra persona o perdonarse sus errores a sí mismo. Tú te sentirás bien por haber ayudado a otra persona y así te recompensarás.

Los ataques premeditados contra otra persona, no se encuentran en la categoría de "errores" y frecuentemente el único alivio sobreviene cuando la víctima te perdona. Si la víctima no está disponible, entonces deberías buscar ayuda profesional y determinar en primer lugar la razón por la cual tramaste ocasionarle daño a otra persona.

No permitir que te deprimas sobre determinado hecho en tu vida futura, es algo mas fácil de decir que hacer. Es importante entender cómo funciona la depresión y darte cuenta de que te mantendrá en la pobreza hasta que logres salirte de sus garras. Si por lo menos recuerdas lo básico, podrás darte cuenta si tú o tus amigos empiezan a caer y podrás revertir la situación o ayudarle a tu amigo, todo por haber tenido la comprensión básica de lo que estaba a punto de suceder.

Lo siguiente es lo que dicen los libros de Psicología acerca de lo que sucede cuando alguien se deprime: típicamente, uno entra en un estado entumecido después de haber experimentado algún trauma. Al desaparecer el entumecimiento, en una semana uno empieza a pensar sobre el suicidio, debido a la culpabilidad. Si uno resiste ese período, siente bastante coraje con uno mismo y luego ese coraje se vuelve contra las personas a tu alrededor. A esta altura, posiblemente nadie quiera vivir contigo y estés sumido en el alcohol, drogas, o estés sin hogar viviendo en un cartón debajo de la autopista. No es probable que entres en este estado simplemente por haber experimentado algún hecho que no se pudo prevenir.

No estoy diciendo que una descomposición mental tan extrema suceda cada vez que te salga algo mal, o cuando se muera tu pez-mascota, pero puede sucederle a un joven que pierde alguna competencia deportiva. Uno casi se muere en ese instante. Para las mujeres, un ejemplo puede ser caerse durante una competición de patinaje sobre hielo, o resbalarse en las barras paralelas después de tantas horas de práctica. Incluso tu entrenador físico ha cometido muchos errores en su camino. Perdónate y avanza. Si otras muchachas pudieran siquiera patinar a tu nivel, estarían en la pista y no se limitarían a hacer de críticas.

Fíjate en la televisión y mira cómo reaccionan los profesionales a sus errores. Ellos tienen que ignorarlo al finalizar el juego, porque no pueden cambiar lo sucedido. Un jugador profesional de béisbol recibe grandes montos por conseguir 1 base cada 3 intentos, consiguiendo un puntaje promedio de 333. Durante las Olimpíadas, el patinador que se cae obtiene el tercer puesto, pero puede lograr el primer o segundo lograr si los otros patinadores también se caen. Recuerda que nunca es demasiado tarde hasta que suena la campana. Considera "nunca rendirte" por pena o sentimiento de culpa. Hay ocasiones en las que es momento de rendirte si te lastimaste o sencillamente no tienes la habilidad de tu oponente, y eso es algo sabio. Considera dar tu 100% hasta que suene la última campana para que tu oponente te recuerde con respeto.

Reservas de dinero

Muchos millonarios se han suicidado cuando su negocio quebraron repentinamente. No pudieron aceptar pensar en regresar a trabajar por un salario horario cuando estaban acostumbrados a considerar billetes de $100 como cambio. Quienes quieran llegar a ser millonarios deben prepararse tempranamente para tener reservas de dinero para emergencias que no toques sin una buena razón. Esta reserva te ayudará a mantenerte tranquilo y probablemente te salvará de arrojarte del balcón de tu penthouse del piso 38 porque has perdido todo. Nunca te rindas. Tú puedes volver de la misma forma en la que lograste tu primer millón. Tomará unos 4 a 5 años más para lograrlo, pero puedes lograrlo. Tener un fondo de emergencia puede ser la base para tu próximo avance hacia arriba. Si caes presa de la depresión, busca los consejos de un profesional o busca el perdón de otra persona.

Logra que otra persona pague tu universidad

Pasemos a un tema más elevado. ¿Cómo podrías ayudar a tus padres a reducir el costo de tu universidad? Empieza este verano, considera ahorrar dinero y muéstrales a tus padres que estás tratando de mantener los gastos de tu universidad bajo control. Quizás ellos estén dispuestos a escuchar tus sugerencias y quizás logren comprar acciones con el dinero que les ahorraste. De esta manera, al momento de tu graduación, no deberán pensar demasiado "en un regalo apropiado" para ti. Todos saldrían ganando, tus padres se quedarían con el dinero si tú no logras graduarte, y tú te esforzarás por lograrlo. Ambos podrán reírse juntos al recordar la competencia. Papá y mamá se sentirán orgullosos de ti, al honrarlos por haberles dejado ser parte de tu experiencia en la universidad. Por esos momentos, todos serán iguales en vez de sólo ser tus padres, como ahora.

Existen muchas formas comunes de ser elegible para becas escolares. Sin embargo, existe otra beca no escolar que posiblemente puedas considerar. Me doy cuenta de que estoy poniendo este tema a consideración de una audiencia adolescente limitada en relación a este mensaje particular, pero si uno o dos de ustedes toman a pecho mi sugerencia, entonces valdrá la pena el espacio que esta información ocupa en este libro. Esta beca se denomina Chick Evan's Caddie Scholarship. Yo me inscribí en la Universidad de Wisconsin con ella en 1954. Es específicamente para los caddies que han trabajado en clubs privados de golf en su localidad por al menos 2 temporadas, y cuyos padres tengas ingresos de bajos a medianos. Ningún campo de golf tiene un cupo que cumplir. Un campo puede recomendar entre 1 a 10 varones o mujeres caddies cada año. Ahora bien, escucha esto: te paga toda tu matrícula, tu alojamiento, y muchos otros grandes gastos de la universidad. Lo único que tienes que hacer es alimentarte por tu propia cuenta. Esto se puede lograr con un trabajo de media jornada como mesero o mesera en cualquier asociación estudiantil. Si quieres añadir otras 10 horas en algún bar local, tendrás suficiente dinero para disfrutar de todos los eventos de la universidad. Mamá y papá pueden viajar a Italia o Costa Rica de vacaciones en vez de sacrificar tanto para mandarte a la universidad. Les estarás ahorrando más de $20,000 por año al hacer esto. Si estas en Illinois tú puedes ir a Northwestern sin tener que pagar los $45.000 por año.

Deberías llegar a ser uno de los pocos estudiantes que tengan más dinero en su cuenta bancaria al finalizar tus estudios universitarios. Esto puede ayudar a tener buenas oportunidades después del colegio como invertir en bienes raíces que necesiten reparaciones, puedes ocuparte de éstas y luego vender los inmuebles obteniendo una ganancia: tú primer paso a llegar a ser millonario. El número telefónico para información sobre esta beca de caddie se encuentra en la sección de referencia, al final de este libro: Western Golf Associations, Golf, IL.

Además del beneficio de la beca, un caddy puede ganar casi siempre unos $75 por día, mientras está al aire libre conociendo a otros jóvenes de su edad a quienes generalmente les gustan los deportes y piensan razonablemente. Algunas de las estrellas de golf empezaron como caddies. Si te interesa este deporte y tu papá no es miembro de un club privado, probablemente no puedas pagar el alto costo de jugar golf, entonces ser caddy puede darte la oportunidad de saber si tienes el potencial de ser jugador profesional. Al mismo tiempo, se te estará pagando por cargar una bolsa sobre tu hombro. Existe una alta probabilidad que recibas lecciones gratuitas de golf de un profesional en el club si le pareces bueno. Sería una situación provechosa para ti.

Otro beneficio es que quizás se encariñe contigo algún profesional del club y te considere como un hijo o hija que nunca tuvo. Como resultado, serás semi adoptado y este miembro podría ser tu guía o instructor para tu primer trabajo cuando termines la preparatoria o la universidad.

En tu propio vecindario

Si no puedes llegar a un campo de golf en tu área, considera las múltiples maneras de ganar dinero cuando no estas en la escuela. Un ejemplo que me impresionó fue el de un joven de 12 años que tomó una carretilla pequeña de niño con 3 bolsas de plástico llenas de tierra y fue de casa en casa en la primavera buscando vecinos que querían que sembrara sus jardines con semillas de vegetales que compró de un catálogo. Acabó ganándose $95 en un solo día.

Hablando de coincidencias, este mismo individuo ahora está sentado en mi oficina este mismo minuto, ya que desde el viernes pasado lo tengo empleado como prestamista en entrenamiento para el negocio de hipotecas. Ahora tiene 21 años de edad y su primer trabajo fue evaluar este manuscrito, el que llegó a ser la edición final que ahora estoy terminando. Este libro será entregado a la imprenta mañana. Él me acaba de sugerir que les mencione a los lectores que cuando él era joven cortaba el césped de todos sus vecinos en su vecindario durante los veranos y se ganaba más de $3.000 cada verano. Él lo recomienda altamente a los lectores, ya que le dio mucho dinero y pudo establecer sus

propios horarios. ¡Éste es el tipo de persona que todos quieren emplear! Considera poner en tu currículum este tipo de experiencia y desarrolla el tema. Demuestra que eres especial y no solamente alguien común.

Aquí están algunas sugerencias:

1. Puedes justificar comprar un auto para ganarte dinero – por ejemplo, recoger y entregar ropa de la tintorería.

2. Puedes pintar casas o cercas.

3. Puedes limpiar ventanas.

4. Puedes coser o remendar la ropa de personas en sus casas.

5. Lavado a presión – Otra forma de ganar muchísimo diner e sir a tu recindad y hacer lavados a presión a los motores de los coches, debajo de la carrcería o arrancar las pinturas viejas a las puertas de los garajes y tambien de los patios. Incluso a los 16 años puedes utilizar esta máquina tan ponderosa. Tu padre puede compratte una máquina a preción de bajo peso que tenga 1400 psi an una ferreteía cercana a tu casa por unos $100. Incluso puedes comprar un en e-bay. Tu padre te enseñara como se utilize de una manera segura y tu puedes ensayar arrancando pinturas vejas alrededor de tu casa. Despúes llevala alrededor de tu vecindad. Es fácil de transportar porque tiene una asa y unas ruedas para trasporte fácil.Lo único que tienes que hacer es conectarlo a la mangera del jardin de tu vecino, apuntar y apreta el gatillo. Las chicas tambien pueden hacerlo porque pesa poco. Es importante llevar puestas las gafas de seguridad porque los fragmentos de los objetos que estas limpiando volarán en mil perdazos alrededor tuyo y necesitas protegerte los ojos.

Tambien, busca una casa de valor en tu vecindad queh tenga ladrillos con mlas hierbas o musgo entre los ladrillos o una calzada o asfalto negro que tenga grietas. Toca a todas las puertas y pregunta si necesitan una buena limpieza profunda para que parezcan nuevos. Con tu máquina a precíon puedes hacer el trabajo en un tiempo record y que la calzada se vea nueva. Tendrás mucho polvo fino en tu ropa, tu cara y el pelo (es muy importante que lleves las gafas de seguridad puestas). Quizás deberías ponerte ropa vieja encima de tu ropa normal así cuando acabes el trabajo pues simplemente te la quitas antes de subirte a tu coche.

Cobra $35 por hora de esa forma podras pagarle a tu

padres en dos dias el equipo que te compró. Una vez que tus vecinos te tengan confianza te llamarán para hacer otro trabajos y a lo major necesitarás emplear a algunos de tua amigos. Piensas en la emoción de ganar tanto dinero y as poder ser independiente. Si quieres ganar $50 por hora entonces pregúntale al cliente si quiere que rellenes las grietas entre los ladrillos o en el asfalto de su casa con arena que contiene sellante en ella. Después de pulverizar levemente la arena con agua, se empieza a endurezer como el cemento y asi prevenir que las malas hierbas vuelvan a crecer entre los ladrillos. Puedes comprar el cemento de arena en tienda como Home Depot o Menards a un buen precio. Puedes cobrarle mas al cliente porque la arena es tuya. Y quien sabe, a lo mejor decides hacerte dentista después de tus 4 años universiratios porque esto de rellenar agujeros te gusto bastante.

Hablando del tema de Odonología recientemente he ido a la Facultad de odontología de la Universidad de Illinois para que unos estudiantes me arreglen los dientes. La idea era experimentar al menos una carrera professional que involverara a estudiantes asi a los lectores de 17-19 años les pueden dar unos puntos de vista si deciden ser proveedores de servicios. En conclusión la Universidad de Illinois tiene una reputación tan excepcional que un graduado puede tener un salario inicial de aproximadamente $ 110,000.00 por año en su primer trabajo. El inconveniente es que la matrícula es de $ 93,000.00 por año.

¿Qué haríamos sin los préstamos estudiantiles? Un beneficio secundario, para mí es que cada visita de trabajo en los dientes consume de 3-4 horas. Los estudiantes y los profesores pasaron el 75% del tiempo en la educación de cada uno de mis dientes individuales y el 25% haciendo trabajos de reparación. Al principio no me gustaba todos los académicos y el consumo de mi tiempo, pero cuanto más me educaban acerca de cada diente en la boca, más me di cuenta de lo que es un servicio de mantenimiento preventivo y generoso que la escuela ofrece. El hecho de que los gastos de reparación fueron 1/3 del costo del dentista barrio, fue una grata sorpresa.

Sobre el tema de divertirse y hacer la máxima cantidad de dinero con la maquina de lavado a precíon, incluso antes de graduarse de la escuela secundaria considerar a tu papá para que te ayude a construir lo siguiente en tu patio trasero:

Dile a tu padre que te compre de la ferretería:

Dos 8' largo 4" x 4" postes

Dos 4' largo 4" x 4" postes

Abrazaderas o tornillos

Una hoja clara de plexiglás de 6' de altura (puede ser cualquier ancho que desee. seis pies es suficiente)

Dos pares de gafas

Instruciones

Conecte el extremo cortado de una sierra del poste de 8' al centro de uno poste de 4' con una abrazadera o los tornillos de algún tipo crear una "T".

Has lo mismo con el otro poste.

Gire al revés para que el poste de 4' este sobre el pasto con el poste de 8' arriba en el aire.

A continuación, has que tu padre conecte ambos postes para que hagan un escudo de plexiglás de una altura de 6 pies (tan amplio como se desee, seis pies es adecuado).

Corte uno o más agujeros en el plexiglás para ser capaz de meter la boquilla de la maquina de lavado a precíon y también te da la capacidad para moverte dos pulgadas de lado a lado del agujero.

Acabas de crear una maquina de lavado a precíon a rango meta.

En el mercado actual, $20,00 por hora es un estimado razonable que podrías recibir al manejar tu propio negocio y encontrar tus propios clientes. Si trabajas para otra persona, busca unos $10,00 por hora, ya que ellos deben buscar los clientes.

El muy importante resultado de haber conseguido tu primer trabajo tiene dos consecuencias. Primero, has aprendido más sobre hacer algo práctico y valioso, como pintar una cochera. Este nuevo talento aprendido puede justificar que cobres más por hora a tu siguiente cliente. Segundo, si hiciste un buen trabajo, podría ser que tu primer cliente te recomiende a su vecino. Solo tienes que pedir que tu cliente te recomiende a quienes posiblemente necesiten el mismo servicio. Entonces usas la misma técnica con tu segundo cliente para conseguir un tercer cliente. Lo más importante es que consigas tu primer cliente. Si puedes venderle a un cliente, puedes venderle a miles de clientes. Si no puedes conseguir un cliente, detente e intenta otra idea.

Para mayor información detallada acerca métodos legales y exitosos para hacer dinero y quizás consejos empresariales, considera ir a la biblioteca o navegar por Internet. Varios autores han escrito bastante sobre el tema. La única desventaja es que muchos de estos métodos dependen de pedir prestado mucho dinero a algún adulto e ingresar en un negocio agresivo con alardes de que ganarás una fortuna en poco tiempo.

A tu edad, tienes muchas prioridades legítimas de la adolescencia que no tienen nada que ver con la disciplina que conlleva una oportunidad de negocio. Sería mejor ir con calma y tranquilo hasta después de haber leído este libro. No debes tener prisa. Lo que te estoy tratando de vender es únicamente la idea de que empieces a pensar sobre el tema y de que empieces a ahorrar dinero. Cuando veas que puedes ahorrar dinero, sentirás el impulso de la inversión y todo se realizará en tu mente.

Si lees en algún periódico que un joven realizó su idea de crear una página en la red y ganó millones de dólares de gente que quería anunciar su productos en su sitio nuevo, trata de no sentir envidia. Por el lado bueno, este individuo poco común debe ser reconocido por haber intentado una aventura sin miedo. Por el lado negativo, este individuo poco común que asume las presiones de manejar un negocio en el mundo adulto tendrá poco tiempo para disfrutar sus últimos preciosos años de la preparatoria.

Los primero dos años de la preparatoria son un período de retención para muchos estudiantes, en el cual las cosas son inciertas y muchos de nosotros pasamos de la niñez a ser pre-adultos. Los últimos dos años de la preparatoria son cuando hacemos amigos para toda la vida y empezamos nuestra independencia de mamá y papá. Si ese individuo poco común que gana un millón a la edad de 16 está demasiado ocupado en dirigir a 6 empleados que quizás tengan dos veces su edad, y tiene que tomar decisiones sobre impuestos al salario, contratos legales, o cuestiones de pleitos, él o ella perderá toda la emoción de estar con sus amigos durante los últimos dos años de la preparatoria.

En cambio, un estudiante que todavía no es rico puede ocupar su tiempo pidiendo una cita al baile de promoción, tener una relación de "amistad de herman o" con sus pares sin necesidad de ser perseguido por el sexo opuesto de manera exagerada a causa de su fama o del éxito en los negocios a temprana edad. La distancia entre ser famoso o alguien común en la vida diaria es muy grande como para comunicarse efectivamente.

Te reitero: honra y respeta al individuo que es tan exitoso en Internet al igual que al joven de 16 años que gana la medalla de plata en las Olimpíadas, y comprende que tu día todavía está por llegar. Considera el precio que ha tenido que pagar el joven de 16 años para triunfar en las Olimpíadas o también el ejemplo del joven de Internet. Ese individuo ha llorado al tener que separarse de sus amigos para dedicar hora tras hora a su práctica. Considera hacerte amigo de esa persona súper exitosa, de la misma manera que quizás te hagas amigo de una persona socialmente retraída. Ambas personas necesitan escuchar a jóvenes de su misma edad que todo saldrá bien aunque no puedan pasar mucho tiempo con los de su clase.

Si haces lo que he sugerido, te sentirás bien contigo mismo. Trata a esos individuos de la manera que te hubiera gustado que se te tratara si fueras tú quien llegó al éxito prematuro, o si naciste con una incapacidad mental que no te permite ser demasiado rápido para agarrar la onda de ciertos chistes. Los dos extremos tienen su ventajas y desventajas. Tú eres lo que eres y eso está bien por el momento. Cuando aceptes este camino, el júbilo de sentirte bien contigo mismo causará que sobresalgas en todo, sean los límites de tu incapacidad o tus talentos naturales.

Capítulo Cinco

"Consejos útiles a medida que maduras"

Consejos Empresariales

Como darte una idea de quien es honesto y muy trabajador y quien es poco confinable según los rasgos facials.

"Eres lo que comes" es la teoría detrás de este tema laamado Macrobióteca. Considera buscar este tema en la computadora. Estó te dara mucha ventaja cuado conozcas a alguien por primera ves.

Aprenderás a interpretar lo que ves en la cara de alguien, si tienen qualidades fuertes o debil cuando se trata de emplearlos en tu negocio. Tambien puedes mirar a tus propios rasgos faciales en el espejo. Quizás decidas cambiarlos, cambiando tu dieta. Cuanto menos contamines tu cuerpo con azúcar y químicos, más guapo te verás con las mujeres, y las mujeres se verán más radiates y con un rostro claro en los ojos de los hombres. Casi todos los libros sobre Macrobiótica tienen fotos y diagramas de rasgos facials para ayudarte a judgar y reconocer a las personas cuando las ves por primera vez. Michio Kushi es un autor de Japon que public los primeros libros y folletos sobre este tema en los E.E.U.U alrededor del año 1970.

Sus diagramas faciales estan basados en trabajos anteriores hace mil años en Japon. Vete a la sección de referencia en las páginas 65-69 de este libro para más información.

Algunos Ejemplos:

1. Mira las cejas de la persona. Si se inclinan hacia arriba la persona es más "YANG" y probablemente muy obstinada. Sin embarago son organizados y cúmplen con el trabajo. Tipo guerrero.

Si las sejas se inclinan hacia abajo, está persona es más "YING" y es más creative. Están probablemente interesados en el arte, artesanía, cocinar y son conscientes de su medio ambiente y de la naturaleza. Es divertido estar con ellos. Suelen ser muy entusiastos y hablan mucho pero no siempre hacen lo que dicen. Tipo que dan cuidados.

La mayoria de nosotros tenemos las cejas planas y uno no puede judgar una forma o otra. Considera escojer un chico de tu escuela que sea el líder de su grupo y otro chico que hable mucho pero sin ácción detrás de sus palabras. Entonces silenciosamente observa sus rasgos faciales.

2. Si la persona tiene el labio inferior grueso eso significa que tiene el inferior debil. El autor de microbiótica dice que debes de estar al tanto que esto significa tener una personalidad débil y egoista.

3. Si una persona tiene la nariz gruesa y se le ven las venas azul ó rojas es porque consume grandes cantidades de azucar refinada como es el alcohol, drogas, caramelos, helados etc... Este tipo de persona tiene dificultad en disciplinarse y pore so suele llegar al trabajo tarde y no pueden quedarse enfocados y por esa razon no acaban sus tareas ó trabajos.

La mayoria de los libros tiene diagramas y rasgos faciales que exhiben todo sobre poder reconocer quien será un asesino multiple o quien será una persona que siempre te dará la razon aunque no sepa de lo que estan hablando.

Otra idea es de obtener un análisis escrito a mano. Antes de conseguir un socio o de emplear a alguien considera gastar $25.oo para recibir una analisis escrito por la otra persona. Lo unico que tienes que hacer es pedirles permiso por escrito para hacerlo.

Los Análisis por Escrito: Para los próximos años cuando necesites empleagar gente.

Como adolescents, yo realize que este tema no les guste ahora. Sin embargo cuando ya entren en el mundo de los negocios es muy caro emplear a alguien que tenga un historial malo y dares cuenta solo despues de una manera dura y realizar que no fue buena idea de haber empleado a esa persona. Intenta recorder este concepto a tu edad, asi cuando tengas 30 años la idea tee s familiar.

La manera de hacer esto es que la persona te de permiso por escrito. Entonces tu utilizes ese permiso y se lo mandas a un profesional que es expert de escritura a mano. Le mandas por correo el original al expert de escritura a mano (busca uno en la computadora) y normalmente al dia siguiente recibes el reporte. El reporte te dará mucha información sobre qué esperar de esa persona. Puedes evitar desperdiciar dinero en emplear a alguien que es un buen conversador y que parece perfecto para el trabajo y darte cuenta mas tarde que esa persona tiene "tendencias" que tut e ves en la obligación de investigar. Esas tendencias pueden ser mentir, robar ó engañar, etc… Tú puedes entonces estar alerta con esas tendencias e investigar a la persona algo mas para asegurarte que vas a emplear a la persona adecuada.

Una buena forma de entender la preción de estas pruebas por escrito es de gastarte $25.oo y mandar una parrafo sencillo y hacer una análisis contigo mismo. El reporte va a destacar la mayoria de tus fortalezas y de tus debilidades. Te sentiras bien contigo mismo por los comentarios positives. Los comentarios que hablan sobre lo que debes mejorar, tú le puedes preguntar a un amigo ó amiga si ellos ven esos "defectos". Esto te puede ayudar a ganar mas dinero sit u sabes cómo te ve la gente. Tú puedes encontrar "Análisis de escritura a mano" en la computadora y es una buena idea pedir referencias via email.

Consejos Personales: La relación Chico – Chica

Pregunta: Por qué el chico ó la chica que te atrae te frusta hasta llegar a llorar a veces?

Respuesta: Son exactamente lo contrario de ti en la mayoría de las cosas y eso es lo que te fascina de ellos. Cada uno de ustedes aporta exactamente lo que el otro no tiene, juntos se "complementan". Se sienten completos cuando estan el uno con el otro. El precio que se paga por esta relación sincera es que jamás se entenderán el uno con el otro.

La intención no es de entenderse el uno al otro. El quiere deportes y tú el concierto. El quiere que vayas con el a un bar Ruidoso con sus amigos del colegio. Tú quieres que el tome clases de baile en el colegio local. No hay final a la agravación y diferencias, pero sin esa persona los dos se sienten incompletos. Con el tiempo los dos aprenden a aceptar los compromisos diarios.

Intenta no confundirte o sentirte amenazado con esta diferencia básica. A medida que aceptas el mundo que te rodea y segues la corriente tendrás la oportunidad de recibir toda la emoción y descubrimiento empezando con tu primer beso. Simplemente relajate y disfruta del viaje.

El asunto es que con la mayoría de las mujeres … no importa lo que tienen… quieren algo Nuevo y diferente (botas ó ropa). Con los hombres… no importa lo que tienen… quieren la misma cosa vieja (una sudadera vieja de 5 años).

Si no fuera por el deseo insistente de las mujeres de comprar nuevos productos (joyas) ó lapiz de labios ó (unos pantalones de mezclilla bien apretados para atraer a los hombres) habría casi cero progreso comercial.

En el cuarto año cuando el egoism se apodera de la relación allí empiezan los argumentos. Ningún consejero te puede ayudar con ese asunto. Estás solo, sin embargo, intenta recorder que la razón de esta fricción y el mal entendido entre ustedes es porque son exactos opósitos. Una vez que entiendan que nunca se van a entender porque son exactos opósitos podrán relajarse y arreglar el problema. Todos los que nos hemos casado hemos pasado por lo mismo que están pasando ustedes hoy dia.

Cuando estas decepciones empiezen a ocurrir, piensa en el pollo que jamás habría salido del huevo de haber sabido lo que el futuro le reservaba. A lo mejor en el peor momento en tu relación te acuerdas del pollo y empiezas a reirte a carcajadas. Eso podría darle una buena pausa al pleito y evitar una discussion verbal fea y ustede dos pueden tener un "lindo momento" en vez de seguir discutiendo.

Sobrevivirán juntos si lo que uno le aporta al Otro estan valoroso como para poder soportar y tolerarse a cada uno. Es más facil decirlo que hacerlo pero intent estar calmado y hablar con tu pareja lo que acabo de decir. A la major acaban riendose con las faltas de cada uno y el problema "horrible" se hará más suave y sera nada más que un compromise ordinario.

Recuerdo que alguien dijo en el pasado que antes de casarse cada socio debería practicar el arte de la empresa (cortejar a la otra persona), pero ya que estás casado que te guste o no, los dos acaban con el arte de compromiso (repirar muy profundo y dejar que la persona diga lo que tiene que decir...quizás aprendas algo).

Puedes ganar una gran cantidad de dinero si entiendes estás diferencias básicas entre hombres y mujeres.

Haz una encuestra verbal con mujeres que conoces sobre el producto que quieres vender. Hasta que la mujer no diga que "si me gustaria comprar eso para mi novio o para mi" no te molestes en comercializar ese producto. Algo le falta.

Resoluer el problema entre los sexos

Miralo de esta forma. **Ejemplo:** tienes 12 problemas en cajas individuals en una estantería y necesitan ser resueltos en un momento particular.

El hombre que sea más (YANG) de los dos tomará el problema que sea más rgente de la estantería y lo hará uno a la ves. El o ella harán todo lo que pueden hacer para corregir ese problema y despues poner la caja de nuevo en la estantería. Despúes tomara el Segundo problema con más urgencia y repetir el proceso. Despúes de eso, está persona se sentira satisfecha y se recomprensará de alguna manera.

El otro socio que es más (YIN) emocional tomará las 12 cajas de un golpe…intentará resoluer los problemas de cada una al mismo tiempo…se frustará y llorará…dejará las cajas tiradas por el suelo y luego se ira de compras o ver que están haciendo los niños.

Intent ver que estó es una "buena" cosa. Si ustedes dos eran super eficientes entonces serían como buenos amigos que se admiran pero que nunca se van ha enamorar. La chispa y la emoción para estar juntos no estaria presents. No se pueden tener las dos cosas.

Varias Reglas para los hombres: (o el más YANG de los dos)

Incluso cuando eres adolescente, aprende a decir, "Si querida y no querida" temprano. Lo unico que una persona Yin quiere es que le des la razón en ese momento. En cuanto ha pasado ese momento. En cuanto ha padado ese momento la persona Yang puede evaluar la situación y hacer lo que piensa que es correcto aunque no sea lo que la persona Yin decidio hace 3 minutos.

La persona Yin que lea estó probablemente se enojara conmigo y quizás piense que soy "chaurinista". Sin embargo para una persona Yang estó es una cosa natural para poder llevar la fiesta en paz y con una conclusion más sensible. Con el tiempo probablemente te darás cuenta de ello. La persona Yin estará pensando en algo nuevo al dia siguiente. La probabilidad es que vean está nueva cosa como algo algo super urgent y importante y ni siguiera recuerdar la ansiedad del dia anterior. Para manterner la paz (tú la persona Yang) solo tuviste que mantenerte callado y intentar entender.

Si la persona YANG es varón, **intenta realizar que solo un "tonto" discute con su novia.** Todo lo que tiene que hacer es echar unas lagrimas y todo tus argumentos lógicos se evaporan. Ella lo único, que quiere es que tú la escuches aunque tú no actues sobre ello. Considera simplemente callarte y escucharla. Quizás aprendas algo si realmente escuchas lo que ella está intentando expresar.

Todo lo que he dicho ha cido con sinceridad y la intención es darles algo a que recurrir cuando haya discusiones entre ustedes. Tú el más YANG de los dos (varón o embra) tundra que morderse la lengua para no explotar pero el dolor de tu lengua mordida es poca cosa comparado al enojo de la person YIN que no se callará y te seguira agrediendo verbalmente. Se nececita verdadera disciplina propia, pero tú el más YANG tienes la responsabilidad de manterner las cosas "calmadas" y no encontrarte absorbido por un argumento que nunca vas a ganar.

Cuando lleges al punto donde él o ella ya no merecen la pena puedes justificar "el siguiente paso" porque le has dado a esa relación todo lo que has podido y ahora es hora de sequir adelante.

Varias reglas par alas mujeres: *(o la más YIN de los dos)*

Si quieres arruinar la relación lo unico que debes hacer es decirle a tu novio que "hacer" en vez de "preguntarle".

Si tú le preguntas si puede hacer algo por ti, esperate a que diga "está bien, lo que tú quieras". Si tú le dices que "haga" algo entonces esperate a un silencio de 3 segundos y luego una semi explosion verbal violent.

El varón adolescente es el "jefe de la familia" (un decir) cuando se trata de tomar decisions. Sin embargo, la embra adolescente ella puede disciplinarse y solicitor cualquier cosa en forma de una pregunata entices ella puede volver "la cabeza" en cualquier dirección que ella quiera. (Este chiste es de la pelicula "Mi gorda boda Griega").

No es facil para un adolescente ser tan disciplinado pero si implementas estas reglas temprano en tu relación, recibiras muy buenos resultados, un 90% de lo que quieres y sin nececidad de levantar la voz.

Si tú le "preguntas" y él te contesta "porqué siempre estás preguntando por cosas, yo tomo las decisions", entonces considera neutralizer tu relación.

Dos tenedores y un pastel

Todos CREEMOS que conocemos a la persona con quien estamos enamorados, y soñamos que podríamos vivir con ellos durante los próximos 60 años, pero nada nos mostrarà la verdadera naturaleza de ellos sin el tiempo.

No hay ninguna prueba real, pero mantenga los ojos bien abiertos. ¿Quién será el primero en comer el último bocado de un delicioso postre? ¿Tu pareja elegirà el último bocado delicioso? ¿O te ofrecerá el último a ti? Un solo acto no es suficiente para descubrir las creencias o el carácter de una persona. Tal vez un evento no es suficiente, puede que tenga una media docena de "postres" durante varios meses para averiguar las verdaderas creencias de su pareja. Estas creencias básicas vienen de la infancia y su pareja nunca va a cambiar. Una persona egoísta siempre va a ser egoísta. Considere la posibilidad de encontrar una persona que pone su satisfacción ante los suyos. Recuerde que va en ambos sentidos, siempre hay que respetar, escuchar y discutir qué es lo mejor para los dos cuando usted está en una relación seria, a largo plazo. Si usted hace esto, su matrimonio sobrevivirá muchos obstáculos.

Tratar a un acosador:

Lo siguiente tiene consejos útiles porque si tienes 14-16 años y no estás completamente desarrollado es muy fastidioso ser molestado y intimidado por los compañeros de clase que son má fiertes y mayores.

Ejemplo:

Supongamos que estás en el primer o segundo año de la prepa y hay un "acosador" que no para de molestarte y intimidarte. Tú tienes que protegerte de la mejor manera que puedas.

Para evitar que el acosador te lesion vas a necesitar alguna forma de defense por ejemplo gritarle, "la única razon por la cual me atacas es para distraer a los demás asi no ven el miedo que tines todos los dias de tu vida".

Claro que quizás el acosador te pegue por haber dicho eso, pero si sobrevives este primer ataque entonces para el proximo puedes gritarle, "me puedes golpear, pero que va pasar cuando lleges a casa y tu padre ha tenido que sacarte de la estación de policia despues de haber pagado una multa de $1500?"

Estás respuestas probablemente harán que el acosador se detenga porqué lo más seguro es que su padre llegue a casa tomado y le pegué a su hijo para desquiciarse con él de su propia íra.

El miedo que tiene el acosador porque su padre tuvo que pagar $1500 para sacarlo de la estación de policia sera suficiente para que se detenga.

Aqui tienes algunas armas verbales adicionales que puedes utilizar para neutralizer al acosador antes de que te ataque de nuevo:

"Mira amigo…soló porque te tardes 5-6 años para graduarte de la prepa eso no te hace major que los demás."

"Mira amigo…tan inteligente como eres y tan tonto como yo soy, yo soy todavía más listo que eres tan tonto como yo."

"Mira amigo…si segues perdiendo el tiempo hacienda tonterias vás a ir a casa llarando."

"Mira amigo…si me segues hacienda daño espera que tu madre se enteré y te quite la propina o tu muñca Barbie."

Este enfoque humano para tu problema inmediato es muy sencible y la amenaza puede terminar alli. Sin embargo, quizás necesites otro enfoque, que necesite un buen par de zapatos para correr. Si encuentras un lugar donde escaparte, entonces hazlo con maxima velocidad y no mires hacia atrás.

Puede ser que el acosador actua como un tipo duro o tipa dura para que tú no veas que en la realidad él vive con mucho miedo y inseguridades por algunas razones. Es todo un encubrimiento. El acosador está simplemente enojado con alguien. Comó tú eres más pequeñito, é o ella te ven como alguien fácil de atacar.

Record Criminal

Niños, han oído sus amigos decir "yo no sabía que estaba haciendo algo malo" cuando fueron arrestados. Antes cuando los adolecentes los arrestaban, la policía los llevaba a la casa y los padres los castigaban. La policía pensaba que eso era suficiente. **Era un insulto para la familia tener una persona quien averguenze el nombre de la familia.** Actualmente, algunos adolecentes quieren tener libertad completa para hacer todo lo que quieran cuando quieran. Considera no juntarte con niños como estos en la secundaria. Tú casi siempre vas a vivir de cheque en cheque cuando tienes un problema en tu record criminal. Nadie va tomar el tiempo para enseñarte nada. Para evitar el castigo de la ley, mejor tú y yo hacemos un trato de **jugar un juego** de nunca romper la ley para dinero de conciertos, carros u otras necesidades. Las reglas del juego son que tú colectes el dinero que mas puedas legalmente y lo guardes en tu vestidor (yo mencione esto al principio del libro) por los próximos 30 días. Cuéntalo. Ahora repite esto por 30 días. Ahora compara los dos totales. Si ves que aumento la cantidad entonces por la primera vez en tu vida tú has hecho una actividad de "metas dirigidas". Vas hacer TÚ quien decide jugar otra vez el juego. TÚ quien decide las reglas del juego. TU quien decide el tiempo para medir éxito y fracaso. TU quien dirige la fundación de tu futuro financiero. Lógicamente, tú vas a estar orgulloso de tus logros. Tú vas a tener respeto para tu mismo. Tú vas a ver que si tú puedes tener éxito en este juego entonces no vas a tener ningún obstáculo financiero que no puedes conquistar. Entonces cuando tengas 35 años y tengas más dinero en tu cuenta de banco del que te imaginaras vas a recordarte del juego del vestidor que fue la causa de tu éxito. La razón es que tú vas usar esta forma para tener más dinero un mes del mes pasado como una meta de cada mes. Tú vas a encontrar formas de hacerlo. Obstáculos se presentaran pero tú los vas a superar como una tormenta. Apenas la tormenta pase tú vas a recoger los pedazos y empezaras otra vez. Si te recuerdas de las películas de Sylvester Stallone "ROCKY" entonces tú sabrás de qué estoy hablando.

Sexting, mensajes de texto y los actos delictivos

Cuando uno es joven tiene muchos caminos para elegir. Usted puede hacer cualquier cosa con su vida. Maestro, banquero, abogado, senador, hasta el presidente -, pero un error, en un instante pueden hacer muchos de esos caminos desaparecen de su horizonte de vida.

Un cargo de sexting, una carga de la posesión, una bebida o mensajes de texto mientras se conduce puede arruinar la vida tuya y de tu familia por muchos años.

Aquí están los hechos: *Todos estos hechos jurídicos siguientes para Sexting, posesión de una sustancia controlada y de mensajes de texto mientras se conduce se han tomado de www.legalmatch.com, palabra por palabra.*

3 formas para tratar a menores como adultos: Hay tres formas comunes en las que se transfiere un caso legal de menores al sistema de adultos para tratar al menor como un adulto. Estos son:

• **Dispensa judicial** - algunos estados les dan a los jueces de menores la facultad de tener el caso de un menor juzgado en un tribunal penal de adultos

• **Discreción fiscal** - algunos estados les dan a los fiscales la facultad de decidir si un menor de edad será juzgado como adulto

• **Exclusión legal** - algunos estados tienen leyes que exigen el caso de un joven a ser juzgado en un tribunal de adultos - estas leyes por lo general basan su transferencia automática en la edad de los jóvenes, la gravedad o el tipo de delito, y el registro previo del menor.

• **Renuncia inversa** - En algunos casos, como el asesinato o la violación, el supuesto es que un menor debe ser juzgado como un adulto a menos que la corte envié el caso a la corte juvenil.

• **Un adulto siempre va ser un adulto** - En algunos estados, si un menor de edad se intentó una vez como adulto, el menor será juzgado como adulto en todos los casos posteriores.

SEXTING:

¿Qué es el sexting? Sexting se define como el acto de transmitir mensajes sexuales explícitos, principalmente por el teléfono celular. Los mensajes contienen fotografías ilícitas o vídeos que muestran a la persona quien los envía. Ellos pueden ser enviados por una persona a otra, y algunas veces pueden ser enviados a varias personas.

Sexting es una tendencia cada vez mayor sobre todo entre los adolescentes que envían mensajes "sext" en relación con citas o coqueteo. La principal preocupación es que si la persona que envía o recibe el mensaje está en la edad adulta, pueden ser condenados por posesión o distribución de pornografía infantil (sobre todo si la fotografía muestra a un menor de edad).

Sexting también puede crear grandes problemas si las imágenes explícitas se obtienen por otras personas sin el consentimiento del emisor, como una persona mayor o un delincuente sexual registrado. Sexting es un desarrollo relativamente reciente, por lo que las leyes que lo rigen son a veces todavía en desarrollo y pueden variar de un estado a otro.

¿Qué estados están procesando los cargos sexting?

Muchos estados imponen sanciones penales por el sexting. Esto se hace siguiendo las leyes de pornografía infantil. Sexting es específicamente ilegal en varios estados, y al menos otros 20 están considerando criminalizar el acto. Algunos estados que enjuician por cargos de sexting incluyen Indiana, Nueva York, Ohio, Pensilvania, Virginia y Wyoming.

¿Qué tipo de sentencia están involucrados en sexting cargos?

Dependiendo de las leyes de la jurisdicción el sexting puede ser un delito ó falta por cargos criminales. Sentencias por cargos de graves delitos pueden tener fuertes multas de $ 500 - $ 1,000 y / o una pena de prisión de al menos un año. Cargos por delitos menores resultan en multas de cientos de dólares y/o un máximo de años en la cárcel.

Una vez más, la principal preocupación en mensajes de sexting es que se aplican las leyes de pornografía infantil. Tales leyes son donde el estado deriva su autoridad para imponer cargos criminales para el acto de sexting. Cargos de pornografía infantil en un contexto de sexting también puede resultar en que el acusado sea colocado en una lista de delincuentes sexuales registrados. En algunos estados, incluso menores de edad han sido colocados en estas listas como resultado de cargos sexting.

¿Qué es la posesión de una sustancia controlada?

Posesión constructiva de una sustancia controlada existe en casos en que no tiene la posesión física de una droga ilegal, pero que tienen ambas:

• El **conocimiento** de la presencia de la droga en o alrededor de su propiedad y **la capacidad de mantener el dominio** y el control sobre él.

Posesión constructiva puede ser exclusiva o conjunta, es decir, ya sea un individuo o un grupo de dos o más personas pueden ser acusadas de manera constructiva de posee la misma sustancia controlada. Por ejemplo, dos personas que viven en la misma casa donde sólo se encuentra una bolsa de marihuana pueden ambos ser declarados responsables de manera constructiva.

Simplemente estar en las proximidades de un medicamento no es suficiente para demostrar la posesión constructiva. Legalmente, se trata igual que la posesión real y permite las mismas defensas.

¿Qué se considera "conocimiento"? Aunque las leyes varían de estado a estado, por lo general, el conocimiento tiene dos componentes:

- Usted debe saber que la sustancia esta en ó alrededor de su propiedad. Este conocimiento no tiene por qué ser real, pero se puede deducir de los hechos o circunstancias incriminatorias.

- Debe conocer o debería haber sabido de la naturaleza ilegal de la droga.

¿Qué se considera la "capacidad de mantener Dominio y Control"? La capacidad de mantener el dominio y el control ha sido interpretada de manera diferente en casi todas las jurisdicciones de los Estados Unidos y el significado a menudo cambia de un caso a otro. En términos generales, esto es cuando la persona sabe que tiene el poder y la intención - directamente, indirectamente o a través de otra persona - para controlar la sustancia. Incluso si usted no tiene la posesión física de la droga, usted puede ser capaz de ganar la posesión física.

¿Las drogas en mi casa o auto son suficientes para demostrar la posesión constructiva? Depende. Recuerda que la proximidad a una sustancia controlada no es suficiente para demostrar la posesión constructiva.

Uso exclusivo Si usted es el único ocupante de la vivienda o el coche en el que se encontró una sustancia controlada, su ocupación exclusiva es suficiente para ejercer el control sobre la sustancia y su conocimiento de su presencia.

Uso no exclusivo Si usted no es el único ocupante de la vivienda o el coche, la posesión es un poco más difícil de probar. Cuando haya más de un ocupante, debe haber pruebas adicionales, tales como hechos o circunstancias incriminatorias, que muestran el conocimiento y control.

¿Qué hechos o circunstancias son incriminatorias? Cada jurisdicción pone una cantidad diferente de peso en los hechos o circunstancias específicas, pero estos son algunos ejemplos de los vínculos comunes entre una persona y una sustancia controlada.

- Los medicamentos están a la vista

- Los medicamentos están con los objetos personales de la persona

- Si está en un automóvil, se encuentran en el mismo lado del vehículo o se encuentran en la proximidad inmediata de la persona

- Si está en una casa, que se encuentran en el dormitorio de la persona

- El comportamiento sospechoso durante la detención

- Los terminales de fumar o parafernalia de drogas

- La propiedad o el control sobre el lugar donde se encuentra la sustancia

Los mensajes de texto mientras se conduce
¿Qué es texto mientras se conduce? Los mensajes de texto mientras se conduce es el acto de leer, ver, escribir o enviar mensajes de texto por teléfono celular mientras se conduce un vehículo de motor. Se trata de una violación de tráfico en movimiento y en algunas jurisdicciones se considera un delito menor. Los mensajes de texto mientras se conduce son sumamente desalentadores, ya que distrae al conductor quien debe de concentrarse en la seguridad vial.

Los estudios han demostrado que los mensajes de texto mientras se conduce aumenta el riesgo de un accidente de vehículo por cualquier lugar desde 2,8 hasta 23,2 veces de lo normal. Por lo tanto, las leyes relativas a los mensajes de texto se orientan más a la prevención en lugar de la recuperación de las pérdidas.

¿Cuáles son las Leyes de texto mientras se conduce? Los detalles de las leyes estatales de mensajes de texto varían dependiendo en la región. Por ejemplo, algunas leyes sólo prohíben los mensajes de texto mientras conducen para las personas menores de 18 años quien tiene un permiso temporal. Consulte con un abogado para obtener más detalles sobre el uso de teléfonos celulares, mensajes de texto y de las leyes de su estado particular.

Actualmente 30 estados y el Distrito de Columbia tienen una prohibición total de toda forma de mensajes de texto para todos los conductores. En 26 de estos estados, la aplicación es primordial, por lo que la policía puede detener a una persona si los ven mandando mensajes de texto mientras conducen un vehículo de motor. En los otros cuatro estados, la aplicación es secundaria, lo que significa es que un agente de policía sólo puede citar al infractor para mensajes de texto, si los han detenido por una violación distinta, como correr en un semáforo.

¿Cuáles son las sanciones por mensajes de texto mientras se conduce? Como se mencionó, las leyes que rigen los mensajes de texto mientras se conduce varían de estado a estado. Sin embargo, el castigo para los mensajes de texto mientras se conduce generalmente incluye una combinación de los siguientes:

• Multas monetarias, éstas pueden ir desde un mínimo de $ 20 hasta $ 500 dependiendo del estado

• Cargos penales - en algunos estados, los mensajes de texto mientras se conduce pueden resultar en cargos de delitos menores (Clase B o C)

• La cárcel o prisión, si el delito ha causado lesiones corporales a otro conductor, la cárcel o la prisión podrá imponerse

La severidad de los castigos aumenta con la reincidencia. Por ejemplo, después de un segundo delito, el juez podrá optar por imponer una multa más alta o una pena de prisión más larga.

Además de las consecuencias jurídicas, otras consecuencias para los mensajes de texto mientras se conduce son:

• Puntos en el registro de conducir

• Suspensión o revocación de los privilegios de conducir

• Clases de seguridad obligatorias

• Confiscación del vehículo, especialmente si hay un gran daño físico como resultado de un accidente

Por último, en algunas jurisdicciones los conductores profesionales y los conductores de autobuses escolares se juzgan con normas más estrictas. Violaciones pueden resultar en multas de más de $ 2.000 para los conductores de camiones y autobuses.

Así que vamos a ser claros, es usted quien debe de mantenerse a salvo y proteger su propio futuro. Yo quería añadir algunos datos que ayudará a considerar que "Perdona", "yo no sabía", o "yo no pienso que" no se tendrán en cuenta en los tribunales y hay que estar atentos a ti mismo.

Sepa quiénes son sus amigos, con quien usted está conduciendo, y habla con tus padres para establecer un plan de contingencia. Tus padres saben que puede fallar, ellos fueron adolescentes, una vez ellos mismos. Si usted está en una fiesta, o con sus amigos y ellos están bebiendo no manejes a la casa con ellos. Si usted tomo una bebida o algo más no conduzca a su casa, llame a mamá o papá o incluso llama a la mamá de tu mejor amigo - la mayoría de ellos vendrá a llevarte a casa. Puede que tenga que enfrentarse a una discusión, un debate serio en la mañana, ó hasta algunas consecuencias, pero será mucho menos que un accidente, la pérdida de la vida ó la pérdida de su propio futuro.

Notes

Te deseo lo major con todos estos problemas de relación…JR

Capítulo Seis
REFERENCIAS

Lecturas seleccionadas/Inversiones/Recursos

Lecturas seleccionadas
You Can Negotiate Anything
(Puedes negociar cualquier cosa)
Por Herb Cohen

Se mantuvo en la lista de Best Sellers durante mucho tiempo. Este libro es educativo e ingenioso. Es un requisito para el estudiante que quiera tener ventaja para ganar negociaciones con sus padres, exageradamente interesados en su entusiasmo juvenil o con la policía que te para por conducir por arriba del límite de velocidad.

Dress for Success
("Vestirse para el éxito")
Por John Molloy

Un viaje educativo sobre cómo tu vestimenta provoca el respeto y atención de los demás. No solamente conseguirás el trabajo en tu primer entrevista, sino que también te ayudará a alcanzar el sueldo más alto dentro de tu empresa. Todo estudiante de drama conoce la forma en que un actor controla a su auditorio según la manera en que se viste. Tú estarás en control de tu entrevista.

Vestirse para tener éxito

Buscá tiendas en tu vecindad en la guía telefonica o en el internet.

Considera:
Trajes por $12.00
Camisas blancas de vestir por $4.00
Corbatas Paisley o simplemete corbatas rojas o azules por $2.00
Zapatos de vestir negros (no marrones) por $15.00
Prendas y zapatos de moda para damas que se ven como nuevos por $5.00

Ponertodo eso jumto de la major manera que puedes y eso sera suficiente y bueno para la entrevista de trabajo aunque te quede algo esto o ancho.

Una vez que eres dueño de tu propio traje, se lo puedes alquilar a tu amigo/amiga para su entrevista de trabajo, y asi empezar un negocio de alguiler de ropa para negocios. Quizás la ropa no te valga pero tu madre puede hacerle unos arreglos. Tambien la puedes usar para el teatro de la escuela o para la boda de tu hermana.

Fuente para ropa hecha a medida

Balani Custom Clothiers
55 West Monroe Street
Chicago, Illinois 60603
Phone 312.263.9003

Esta empresa familiar me ha vestido a mi y a mi famila en trajes y ropa especializada desde 1962. Tienen fuentes de prendas de vestir, materiales y confección que no son fácilmente disponibles en las tiendas. Sus precios son satisfactorios porque toda la ropa es hecha en ultramar.

Acciones Especulativas Seleccionadas

Renuncia: *nada de lo que sigue son recomendaciones para compra acciones. Esto es un mero ejercicio académico para involucrarte en lo que se entiende por una acción "símbolo" o la importacia de la "banda de fluctuación" por lo que cuando usted hable con los corredores de bolsa, tundra una buena idea de lo que está hablando.*

LEEP, Inc. (conocidos antes como Leading Edge Earth Products. El nombre fue combiado a LEEP a finales del añ 2004.)

Símbolo de cotización LPPI
Página de web www.leepinc.com
La planta de fabricación en Williamsport
Pennsylvania USA

Esta empresa manufactura un panel a prueba de fuego con aislamiento para el montaje de casas. Ellos dicen que carga pesada, de peso liggero, huracán, moho aguanta de termitas y prueba de roedores. De alega que es recistente a los terremoros con un factor de aislamiento similar a una hielera y se fuede montar por el mismo costo que una casa hecha con varillas de madera en menos de 40% del tiempo. El precio de las acciones en Abril 2010 estaba en el rango de $.02 por acción. Estas acciones pueden subir a $1.00 como pueden bajar a un centavo. Me gusta porque tiene la respuesta al suministro de los nuevos materiales para la reconstruccción de lugares como Nueva Orleans y Mississippi despues del ultimo huracán y todos los futuros.

El govierno de los Estado Unidos está actualmente utilizando este product como el unico product aprovado para la solicitud unica de un edificio que tiene una temperature constant muy útil para comprobar correo que llega a los Estados Unidos, que puede contener las bomabas de correos o virus. Considera esta una acción muy, muy especulativva, con un future de mil millones de dólares lo mismo que Microsoft en 1975. Yo pienso que el 30% de los lectores de este libro van a vivir en una casa construida sobre LEEP-CORE los próximos 20 años.

Northern Dynasty Minerals
Símbolo de contización NAK
Páagina web www.pebblepartnership.com
Oficina principal en Vancouver British Columbia, Canada.
Número de telephono: 907.339.2600

Se rumorea, que a principios del año 2001 descubrieron la mina de ora más grande del mundo y la segunada mina de cobre más grande del mundo. La mina está localizada aproximadamente a 75 millas al oeste de Cook's Inlet a través de Homer, Alaska y 16 millas de Iliamna, Alaska. El precio de las acciones era aproximadamente $9.00 por acción. Considera estas acciones una buena compra y una especulación mediana.

Lecciones básicas sobre cómo elegir para comprar una acción

El proceso de análisis: por ejemplo, productos.

Haz una lista de productos que utilizes todos los dias:

- Que product le gustan – otros adolescents están utilizando y gustando este mismo product?

- Escoje tus tres productos favoritos

- Investigalos en el internet. Bloomburg.com es una fuente para saber quien hace ese producto.

- Obten su símbolo de cotización.

- Busca el costo de una cuota

- Comprueba una vez por semana com ova la acción – tú "inversion imaginaria".

No te cuesta nada hacer "comercio de papel" en el computador. Tus amigos y tú pueden hacer un juego y competir por algún premio como un billete de $10.00 para ver quien puede llevarse $50,000.00 de dinero falso que el programa de tú computadora te da para que se aumente más allá de los demás participantes. Simplemente haz que tu padre te presente a un corridor de bolsa como Ameritrade, Scott Trade, Monster Trade o E-Trade y poner $200.00 en una cuenta. Después no toques los $200.00 y solamente usa el "comercio de papel" para divertirte y asi aprender como funciona el sistema commercial.

Fuentes de monedas de oro y plata o ETFs

Monedas de oro y plata
Monex: 1-800-752-1400
Certified Mint: 1-800-528-1380
Trade Monster: 1-877-598-3190 #2- ETFs
Ameritrade: 1-800-669-3900 - ETFs

Si deseas evitar el inconveniente de guardar los metales en alguna caja fuerte, considera comprar oro y plata en el American Stock Exchange bajo el símbolo de GLD o SLV. Entonces sólo retendrías certificados de acciones en papel garantizados con el metal actual; es decir, lo mejor de dos mundos. El valor aproximado del oro en de Abril de 2010 es de $1100.00 por onza. El valor aproximado de la plata es de $18.00 por onza.

Algunas personas piensan que el oro puede llegar a $1600.00 en los próximos 4 años y la plata a $30.00. trten de enternder que los dólares de papel en su bolsillo son compatibles o respaldamos por el metal. El metal respaldado es la parte valiosa y los dólares de papel están imprimidos solo para su conveniencia porque el metal pesa mucho para llevar a todas partes. Ameritrade (1800.669.3900) y Trade Monster (877.598.3190 ext 2) tienen una commission fija en el rango de $10 por el comercio en el internet.

Becas universitarias para caddies

Llama a la Western Golf Association
1 Briar Rd., Golf, Illinois 60029
1.847.657.7556

Esta beca está disponible para caddies que trabajan en campos de golf exclusivos y es como vivir en una fraternidad de las universidades del estado. Uno también puede elegir a qué escuela asistir si existe una razón suficiente. De cualquier manera, estarás ahorrándole $20,000 por año a tus padres en gastos escolares. Ellos te podrán orientar con los campos de golf en tu localidad que estén ofreciendo el programa.

Ellos pagan escuelas como Northwestern en Evanston, Illinois a $45,000.00 por la matrícula de un año, vivienda y dinero para otros antículos o para una escuela del estado de approximadamente $20,000.00 al año. Tienes que estar en el cuarto superior de tu clase. Tus padres tienen un salario modesto. Tienes que ser un caddie durante dos veranos y hacer aproximadamente 150 rondas. Considera echarle un vistazo hacienda primero una llamada.

Macrobióteca

Buscalo en el internet, tineda de libros o en la bibliteca. Uno de los autores de prominencia: Michio Kushi. Esta asignatura trata de los 1000 años de arte Japonés del diagnostic de las características humanas para predecir el future de la salud y los patrones de comportamiento de los individuos.

El reconocimiento de las nuevas industrias Millionarios

Quizás quieras obtener un trabajo de nivel de entrada después de tú graduación:

Dos ejemplos:

Células madre: estas empresas son capaces de tomar las células humanas de una sección rota o desgastada de un cuerpo humano y fabricar un cultivo de laboratorio de fluidos. El cultivo del liquid entonces se inyecta en la zona herida o desgastada y hace crecer nuevas células en cadenzas largas con cada cadena creciendo más brotes al igual que una planta de jardin. Esto restaurará el area dañada o desgastada teoricamente hasta su fuerza juvenil original. Una vez inyectada en el cuerpo, el cultivo del liquid "buscará y encontrará su propia fuente" en el sitio de la zona con el problema. Por eso, el nombre…células inteligentes…imagina lo que esto significara para los deportistas, victimas de acidentes de coche, Dolores de espalda debido a rupture de discos, ect…cuando este evento ocurra en 6-8 años, considera vender tu acciones en la industria farmacéutica debido a que sus ganancias van a sufrir porque los analgésicos ya no serán populares como alguna vez lo fueron.

El diagnostic de preimplantación genetic y células madres: Investigadores yah an perfeccionado la capacidad de diagnosticar e informar a los padres si un óvulo fecundado humano feminine del niño aún por nacer tundra síndroma de down, autism, alzeimer, cancer, etc. El costo normal es de aproximadamente $1000.00.

Que yo sepa, la empresa actual que es la más grande y avanzada, se llama Reproductivee Genetics Institute y esta localizada en 2825 N. Halsted Street, Chicago, Illinois 60657, telefono 773.472.4900.

Combustibles Bio Diesel: Empresas en esta industria tienen un nuevo producto quémico para dissolver casi cualquier tipo de vegetación o el suelo de los árboles, luego se fermenta la mezcla para emitar humos, que a su vez producen Etanol. Solía ser que sólo los granos como el maíz o la soja podia ser utilizado. Imagina si sólo utilizamos el 30% o menos de la gasoline actual y todo, desde la hierba cortada a la vegetación de la selva produce el otro 70% con el mismo precio o menos de la gasolina.

Acuerdate de estas dos industrías cuando eventualmente vas a buscar un trabajo a tiempo completo.

Capítulo Siete
"Más allá de nuestras fronteras"

"Aprovecha una oportunidad y riega la semilla. Espera y ve dónde te llevará".

Adolescentes en otros países

Esta sección es para los adolescentes que viven en un país del tercer mundo o un país dirigido por un dictador. El estudiante norteamericano corriente le pondrá poca atención a lo que tengo que decir porque está muy lejos de la libertad personal que disfrutamos en los Estados Unidos. En vez de no incluir esta sección en el libro pensé que a algunos de ustedes les gustaría saber que a jóvenes de otros países se les evita poder alcanzar su potencial completo porque no se les da el "derecho a elegir". Tienen que hacer lo que se les manda hacer, o no podrán conseguir un trabajo. Si hablan en público acerca de esto se les echa en prisión.

Nosotros en los Estsdos Unidos hemos crecidos siendo alentados a experimentar con todo para intentar mejorar el mundo a nuestro alrededor. El sistema de pensamiento detallado en este libro funciona bien en los Estados Unidos, Canadá, Inglaterra, muchos países de Europa y algunas otras naciones prominentes en otros continentes del mundo. La razón porque funciona es porque los políticos de las naciones desarrolladas entienden que pueden beneficiarse de las ganancias de los pequeños empresarios exitosos, en la forma legítima de impuestos, lo que funciona mejor que la extorsión o la intimidación.

Los estudiantes que viven en países del tercer mundo o en sociedades semi-modernas donde la corrupción y los sobornos son normales, ven que los políticos locales hacen todo lo posible por confiscar una buena porción de las ganancias para sí mismos cuando uno comienza a ser exitoso. Si no les pagas tributo, tu casa y tu oficina pueden quemarse por completo en la oscuridad de la noche, en un aparente accidente.

A los políticos que piden sobornos no les importa nada tratar de construir una base social de estudiantes que puedan contribuir a un país más fuerte y mejor en el cual vivir. Te presionan sin descanso para que les des más y más dinero, justificándose en que si ellos no lo hacen, otro político te lo exigirá, por lo que razonan que deben conseguir todo lo que puedan de ti antes de que les gane otro político.

No tengo una respuesta acerca de cómo puede uno actuar con ese sistema tribal en su país, el cual lleva más de 1000 años. Sin embargo, sí puedo, darte ánimo, como individuo, a que trabajes en medio de la corrupción sin ser tú mismo corrupto. Considera dedicar tus energías en llegar a ser el líder dentro de la organización política corrupta y deja de lado por unos años el concepto de convertirte en millonario.

Cuando llegues a esa posición de líder entonces podrás cambiar gradualmente ese sistema corrupto desde adentro. En ese sentido, lograrás ser millonario en aspectos que afectarán de manera positiva a todos en tu país. Al morir los políticos actuales, tú podrás subir a la cima. Entonces tendrás la opción de ser igualmente corrupto o podrás empezar haciendo tu contribución para convencer a los poderes que te rodean de que una clase media de empresarios debe ser apoyada y de que no se roben sus ganancias por medio de la extorsión. Tu puedes fijarte como objetivo principal llevar a que tu país facilite los negocios y hacer más fácil que los individuos obtengan licencias de negocios sin tener que pagar sobornos. Puedes remitirte a creencias tribales, ritos, y privilegios de los tiempos pasados para abrir camino a normas rectas para el comercio entre comprador y vendedor, junto con protección a la comunidad de negocios para que no tengan que pagar tributo a los políticos locales para recibir "protección".

Quizás tu generación nunca vea los resultados de tus buenos esfuerzos. Tú, sin embargo, tendrás la satisfacción de saber que hiciste el intento de cambiar las cosas para mejor y, de esa forma, serás honrado. Dentro de todo lo bueno que hagas, es muy posible que encuentres resistencia. Quizás hasta sufras violencia física bajo las órdenes del dictador local. Sin embargo, conseguirás un modo de vida superior al de los demás, por haber hecho el esfuerzo de involucrarte en el sistema político actual y hacer un cambio. Te deseo buena suerte.

Notes

Capítulo Ocho

Resumen

El Futuro

Espero que hayan disfrutado esta aventura gozosa a través de este libro. Ahora, o en veinte años a partir de hoy, cuando seas una persona rica, me podrás contar lo que te gustó o no te gustó de este libro. Apreciaría recibir tus comentarios por e-mail:

JR@TheFutureBelongsToMe.com

Quizás tus comentarios puedan mejorar el mensaje que quiero traducir a nuevos adolescentes que están por venir. Sería tu contribución según la Regla 2: "No puedes ayudar a alguien sin ayudarte a ti mismo". Mira inmediatamente después si no te sientes tan bien contigo mismo por haber usado tu imaginación para sugerir algo para ayudar a un preadolescente nuevo por venir y harás en ese mismo momento algo para recompensarte. Tal vez iniciarás tu primer libro, el cual has estado pensando en escribir hace ya un tiempo, pero no has podido poner tus ideas en papel.

Notes

Capítulo Nueve
DESPUES

"Guía para el Millonario:
cómo volver a ser un Adolescente"

Mi Próximo Libro

Ya estoy pensando en mi próximo libro. El título será "La guía para el Millonario: cómo volver a ser un Adolescente." Un resumen del libro es que muchos millonarios de más de 40 años ya "han hecho y visto todo". Algunas veces les sobreviene el aburrimiento y extrañan los desafíos de una nueva conquista. Mi primera idea es encender su pasión juvenil y ayudarles a duplicar o triplicar su fortuna siendo profesores y conferencistas de media jornada.

Universidad de Millonarios

Mi segunda idea es que unos 200 millonarios donemos un millón y con eso compremos (o que se nos donen) varias fábricas o bodegas grandes y vacías en áreas urbanas decaídas, y así dar inicio a la Universidad de Millonarios. (En Chicago, he identificado un sitio al este de la avenida Cicero y la avenida Grand). El interés de los fondos permitirá correr con los gastos y el capital no se tocará sin el consentimiento del 55% de los participantes para la expansión o gastos grandes. De esta manera, si quiebra todo, a todos se les regresará su millón invertido.

Sólo se invitará a millonarios a enseñar o dar conferencias en un programa rotativo. Cada participante será asignado para una conferencia al menos una vez al año. El pago será $1.00 por asistir y los gastos aproximados para el estudiante serán de $1.00 por lectura. Las experiencias individuales de cada millonario será un libro sin escribir sobre cómo ganaron y perdieron grandes cantidades de dinero. En un estilo natural, esto se expandirá a la consejería individual a jóvenes empresarios. Convivir entre hombres y mujeres ricas y disfrutar de una cerveza con estudiantes después de clase puede "provocar" una nueva meta y cambiar por completo la actitud de otros a su alrededor.

Quizás algunos se sientan más "completos" al sentir de nuevo el júbilo y la risa que tuvimos en la preparatoria o en la universidad. Quizás algunos de ustedes encontraran "alguien significativo", como un compañero de vida personal, quien aprecia que tu mente esté constantemente enfocada en cuestiones financieras, en vez de criticarte por esto, porque las prioridades de esa persona son las mismas.

También, viendo el lado positivo, sospecho que toda persona con mente de negocios que haya leído el resumen precedente ya estará tomando su teléfono celular y llamando a su agente de bienes raíces para comprar la propiedad barata en la zona de la Avenida Grand que mencione arriba. Una universidad revitalizará un área deteriorada y creará muchos millonarios en varias ciudades en los Estados Unidos. Así es como legítimamente puede funcionar y quizás tú seas uno de ellos. Si algunos de ustedes millionarios que lean este libro quieren contribuir ideas o punto de vista, podría ser bueno para todos nosotros. Por favor ponerse en contacto conmigo en el e-mail a:

JR@TheFutureBelongsToMe.com

Notes

Notes

Capítulo Diez
METAS INDIVIDUALES DESPUÉS DE LEER ESTE LIBRO

Escribe tus metas personales, mejoramientos e ideas para la inversion en una revista.

Primer semana: _____

_____

_____

Primer mes: _____

_____

_____

Primer año: _____

_____

_____

Cinco años: _____

_____

_____

Sugerencias a conciderar para mejorar:

Actitud – Hazte la pregunta, "¿Cómo puedo ser una mejor persona?"

_____
_____
_____
_____
_____

Responsabilidad Civil – ¿Puedo donar mi tiempo/habilidades para una buena causa?

_____
_____
_____
_____
_____

Apariencia – Haz una lista como puedes mejorar la impression que otros tienen de ti asi los empleados potenciales te veran favorablemente en vez de "solo un niño buscando trabajo."

_____
_____
_____
_____
_____

Fuentes de inversiones potenciales

Productos – Haz la lista de productos que usas todos los dias:

_____

_____

_____

_____

¿Qué productos te encantan? – Existen otros jóvenes que usan y aman el mismo producto?

_____

_____

_____

_____

Escoje 3 – escoje tus 3 productos favoritos. Investígalos en Internet. Averigua sus símbolos en la bolsa de valores. Investiga cuánto cuestan sus acciones. Sigue el valor de 100 acciones, "sólo en papel". Averigua su valor cada semana y determina los resultados como si realmente hubieras comprado las acciones – comó estubo tu inversion? No te cuesta nada hacer "comercio de papel" en el internet. Tus amigos y tú pueden hacer un juego y competir por algún premio como un billete de $10.00 para ver quien puede llevarse $50,000.00 de dinero falso que el programa de tú computadora te da para que se aumente más allá de los demás participantes. Tu padre te puede presentar a un corridor de bolsa como Ameritrade, Scott Trade, Monster Trade o E-

Trade y poner $200.00 en una cuenta. Después no toques los $200.00 y solamente utiliza el "comercio de papel" para divertirte y asi aprender como funciona el sistema commercial.

Mantén un registro de cómo haces en tu diario.

¡Felicitaciones!

– SEGÚN MI OPINIÓN –

SI HAS LLEGADO A ESTE PUNTO EN EL LIBRO, TIENES TODA MI ADMIRACIÓN. MI PENSAMIENTO EST QUE PROBABLEMENTE SERÁS UN GANADOR EN CUALQUIER OCUPACIÓN QUE ESCOJAS.

Notes

Apéndice

Breve explicación sobre metafísica

Apéndice Uno

La razón por la que este tema se ubica al final de este libro quizás no tenga mucho sentido para la mayoría de ustedes esto no sea muy significativo. A pas 17 años tu celebro está demaciado "empapado" para manejar el reto. Por esa misma razón los curzos de la segundaria no son enseñados en la primaria. Sin embargo tiene mucha significancia para mi. Quiero compartirlo contigo porque este tema es la base de mis logros financieros. En actividades diarias, quizás se comprenda el aspecto de su significado al decir que me ha guiado para pasar de ser un hombre corriente de 50 años al llega a ser uno de 64 años que en el año 2000 gané el 10mo lugar nacional, representando a Illinois, en las 400 metros de las Olimpíadas Senior con un tiempo de 1:136, ganando también la medalla de oro y medallas de plata en la carrera de 200 metros en Illinois. También me ha guiado para "descubrir" cómo ganarme la modesta fortuna que he acumulado durante los últimos 20 años.

Este tema es un maravilloso reto para cualquier adolescente que, con pluma en mano (ahora computadora), quiere empezar a escribir su primer libro. Considera este tema como un "campo de entrenamiento" – un lugar donde empezar, ya que demanda no sólo excelentes dotes periodísticas, sino también una investigación sobre temas accesibles que darán vuelta en tu mente y te llevarán en varias direcciones.

Cuando hayas pasado un año estudiando el tema, estarás dividido en campos opuestos que te empujarán a un estado de humildad. Después de esto, cualquier otro tema que escojas para escribir será un alivio en comparación a la metafísica. IDEAS contra CREENCIAS, es esencialmente el tema de la metafísica. Puedes ganar prominencia dentro de tu grupo si entiendes estos conceptos opuestos, dado que cada adulto, a su propia manera, está buscando la verdad en cuanto tal, porque existe en primer lugar.

Considera utilizar la biblioteca o Internet para investigar la definición de la Realidad y la No Realidad. Encontrarás que las cosas que son realidad nunca cambian y que las cosas que no son reales varían constantemente. Nota que todo en el mundo material está ajustándose o expandiéndose constantemente, y entonces cae en la definición de no ser real.

Imagina la reaccion de tus amigos cunado les digas que tu coche o tu cuerpo no son reales. No querran oíque todos los objectos materiales que puedes ver son simplemente illusions o reflecciones de ideas. Si es invisible como son las ideas entonces es REAL. Tienes que guardae esas observaciones para ti mismo o tus amigos van a pensar que eres raro aunque estés diciendo la verdad.

Tú tendrás que escoger cual de los dos opuestos piensas que es el camino a seguir.

Una será que tu cuerpo es sólo un disfraz que usarás aproximadamente desde los 6 a los 60 años y cuando se acabe (tú morirás) nada cambiará. Tu conciencia solo recibe un nuevo disfraz en la forma de un bebé en alguna parte del universo.

La segunda opción será las enseñanzas de las religiones populares que enseñan que cuando tu cuerpo muere, tu mueres.

La próxima vez que estés en una cita con un grupo y la conversación se empiece a apagar, considera sacar este tema y empieza a darle al grupo cosas básicas, de la mejor forma que puedas. Entonces échate hacia atrás y observa cómo saltan los cohetes. Puede ser divertido y nadie puede comprobar que uno tiene razón o está equivocado.

Apéndice Dos
Un mensaje de despedida por J. R.

Los editores con los cuales he trabajado al escribir este libro me animan a redactar una biografía de mis 70 años. Mi experiencia probablemente es tan gustosa (mis altas) y también terrenal (en mis bajos) como la de cualquier otro ser humano. Realmente no son importantes las experiencias que componen "mi historia". Lo que es importante es lo que forma "tu historia". Como adolescente tienes una energía sin límite. Aunque tu energía esté mal dirigida debido a un ambiente inconveniente en tu hogar o por alguna tragedia que te haya asustado, todavía puedes dar lo mejor de ti, como una planta que florece y llegar a ser un adulto maduro. Date permiso en dejar que salga todo, sin retenerlo. Si te dedicas siempre a lo "bueno", tú estarás del lado correcto y tendrás suficiente dinero, un compañero o compañera del alma y, lo más importante de todo... Una familia con la cual estar.

La gente que está en prisión o comete suicidio frecuentemente lo hace porque se siente "siempre en soledad" y no forma parte de ninguna tribu. Aun dentro de una familia disfuncional -y todos tenemos algunos miembros excéntricos-, ésta se une y se aceptan todos los problemas sólo para sentir "que son parte de algo". Todos necesitamos ser "entendidos" y las personas más adecuadas para hacer eso son aquéllos con quienes andamos. El punto al cual estoy llegando es que, sin importar, cuán bajo llegues, tú puedes salir de ese estado siendo parte de un grupo que te acepte por lo que eres. Cuando eso sucede, tu sentido de confianza y energía burbujean con el entusiasmo por vivir. Entonces, podrás determinar el camino que recorrerás hacia el logro económico. Más importante aún, trata de gozar la libertad y la emoción de poder ser tú mismo. Lo que yo describo es lo que me ha sucedido a lo largo de los últimos 70 años y algún día ustedes estarán estimulando con entusiasmo a tus hijos o nietos. Puede ser que con algunas pocas palabras reconfortantes logres una diferencia en la vida de otra persona, al igual que yo estoy intentando hacer una diferencia en tu vida.

Si te gusta lo que has leído y tiene sentido para ti, compártelo con tus amigos y luego vende este libro en tu vecindario para que ganes unos dólares más por semana, en vez de trabajar por un sueldo mínimo en algún otro lugar. Puedes comprar este libro en cantidades de cinco (5) en Internet por aproximadamente lo mismo que pagaría una gran tienda. Entonces, puedes vender el libro al mismo precio por el que lo venden las tiendas grandes.

Lo que sucederá es que ya no tendrás que trabajar detrás de la barra en algún café, escuchando a gente que hace su pedido mientras tus piernas están cansadas y sólo deseas sentarte. Quizás puedas dejar tu trabajo de cambiar aceite en algún taller y evitar andar con uñas que nunca pareces estar limpias. ¿Por qué no ganarte una mayor cantidad de dinero simplemente manejando tu bicicleta por tu barrio, tocando de puerta en puerta (vístete adecuadamente), preguntando a los dueños de casa si no les gustaría un regalo para sus nietos, para cumpleaños, graduaciones, o para Navidad?

Si has leído o estudiado el libro personalmente, puedes contarles a quienes vienen a la puerta lo significativo que fue para ti y cómo puede enriquecer la vida que brindan a sus hijos y nietos, de la misma manera que ha enriquecido tu vida. De repente, habrás empezado un negocio con un producto que tú mismo has comprado. ¿Qué tal serían las universidades o preparatorias y sus bibliotecas o librerías como un lugar para preguntarles si te compran el libro para satisfacer las necesidades de sus clientes? Un punto que se puede destacar a los profesores de Español es que se puede usar como ayuda. Ellos pueden usar este libro para compararlo con el otro y sospecho que el tema es más interesante que lo que se encuentra en otros libros.

¿Qué tal un centro de mayores donde puedes hacer tu presentación durante sus noches de actividades? Algunos posiblemente se encuentren en sillas de ruedas y les encantaría comprar un regalo para sus nietos sin tener que dejar la casa, sería una verdadera ventaja.

Considera hablarle a los dueños de tiendas que venden mercancía de alto valor, como joyerías, autos, abrigos de pieles, etc. Sugiérele al dueño que puede conseguir futuros clientes al regalar este libro a cualquier cliente que compre algo que rinda ganancias por encima de $1000. ¿Por qué no pedir a los agentes de bienes raíces que regalen el libro a sus clientes con las ventas de casas? Deberían hablarnos para tomar el primer pedido y nosotros anotaríamos que es un vendedor a comisión, junto con su dirección. La oficina o agente individual puede colocar su propia calcomanía o logotipo en la encuadernación del libro para recordar a sus clientes de su existencia para futuras compras o referencias. La idea detrás de regalar este libro a sus clientes ricos no es porque ellos lo necesiten o vayan a leer este libro. Ellos se lo pueden pasar a los jóvenes que conozcan, lo que los hará sentirse bien consigo mismos. Es el mismo sentimiento que sienten tus padres al regalarte algo que para ti significa mucho. A las personas ricas les satisface compartir o enseñar a personas jóvenes a trabajar más sabiamente y ahorrar dinero, así como ellos acumularon sus propias fortunas.

La idea es que los compradores ricos entienden cómo ganar grandes cantidades de dinero con sus negocios propios Sólo mencionar la palabra "millonario" obtiene su atención que de la misma manera a obtendría tu atención si mencionara algún grupo de rock. Posiblemente vean el valor inmediato de que sus nietos o hijos lean el libro. Quizás hasta ellos mismos quieran leer el libro porque tiene que ver con cómo hacer una ganancia y ése es el tema sobre el cual piensan todo el día, de todos modos.

    Considera llamar a todas las fábricas en tu vecindario. Pregúntale al jefe si le gustaría regalarle a sus empleados un libro esta Navidad. A los empleados posiblemente les gustaría pasarle el libro a sus hijos para que logren ser más exitosos que ellos. Sugiérele al jefe que sus empleados tendrán una mayor consideración y un mayor respeto por él porque el regalo influye de manera favorable en los hijos de sus empleados. Menciónale al jefe que sus empleados pueden retribuirle por considerar que sus hijos y sus familias aprendieron a ayudarles a recortar sus gastos e incrementar su producción. Todos salen ganando. Todo, como consecuencia de que aprovechaste una oportunidad e invertiste una pequeña porción de tu tiempo sin ninguna garantía de éxito financiero para hacer que el jefe se de cuenta de que el libro será exitoso. Esto es como empezar tu propio negocio. Antes de zambullirte, primero pruebas el agua con tu dedo grande del pie, y determinas si esta fría o caliente. Puedes procurarte uno o dos clientes en tu descanso de almuerzo, si puedes venderlo a un solo cliente, puedes venderlo a cien. Si no puedes vender ninguno, entonces detente y continúa con tu trabajo a sueldo.

    Imagínate cuán bien te sentirás contigo mismo cuando el jefe te llame para solicitarte más libros (asegúrate de dejarle una tarjeta con tu nombre y teléfono), porque aprecia que hayas pasado a verlo, ya que a sus empleados les gustó la idea de tener una guía que pudiera enseñarles a sus hijos cómo superar el nivel de pobreza en el cual actualmente viven. De repente el trabajador de fábrica no muy educado, se torna una fuente de conocimiento para sus hijos. Esto probablemente conmoverá hasta las lágrimas a alguno de estos padres que por fin ha logrado hacer algo por sus hijos además de simplemente brindarles lo mínimo en comida y vivienda. Recuerda: tú fuiste quien puso todo el asunto en movimiento.

Quizás uno de tus padres tiene buena orientación para los negocios y puede ayudarte con ideas adicionales para hacer ventas en tu vecindario. Quizás los dos pueden pasar un poco de tiempo en este proyecto y renovar la amistad que tuvieron antes de que entraras a la adolescencia, mientras tú has sido temeroso al ser visto con sus padres, por temor a lo que dirán tus amigos.

Asumiendo que este libro tiene éxito en el mercado, podremos formar una empresa donde el 90% de los empleados sean adolescentes. Ellos pueden encontrarse alrededor de todo el mundo, con la oficina central en Palatine, Illinois. Sobre la base de medias jornadas, los empleados podrían manejar las computadoras, el mercadeo e intentar solucionar cualquier problema que surja (algunos adultos pueden tomar las riendas si el problema resulta demasiado grande). La idea sería como "Logro Juvenil" pero con balas reales. Probablemente, no sería muy profesional y se verían pocas ganancias, pero sería divertido ver a un joven de 17 años tener que mantenerse en pie por primera vez.
Esencialmente, sería como un laboratorio para los interesados en negocios. Sin importar las ganancias, si la idea tiene éxito en vez de caerse, imagina los amigos que harás y las oportunidades que tendrás de viajar con otros jóvenes de Europa, Medio Oriente, Asia y América Latina, quienes también serían empleados.

Los buenos resultados llegan en diferentes formas. Puede ser que ni siquiera vendas un solo libro, pero también podría ser que conozcas a tu primer amor en el proceso de visitar a clientes potenciales. Lo peor que podría suceder si no vendieras un solo libro es que regales los libros que te sobren a un primo menor o a un vagabundo en la calle. Quién sabe, quizás tú seas la razón de que un vagabundo que lea este libro se perdone por haber cometido errores o ser responsable de una tragedia y que todavía se sienta culpable, termine reintegrándose a la sociedad y consiga un trabajo.

Considera mandarme un correo electrónico. Podemos discutir el tema de conseguir clientes sobre la base de tu experiencia en el campo y yo puedo pasarles a otros jóvenes tus historias de éxito, si ellos no van agarrando la onda. Tu historia de éxito podría darles una visión claro que perpetuaría todo el concepto de las reglas 1 y 2.

Se ha dicho suficiente y ya es momento de que te acuestes y apagues la luz. Como un sincero final, necesito que contestes una pregunta primordial. ¿Cuántos lectores se dieron cuenta de que todo lo que hice es escribir un libro donde explico a los jóvenes, en un lenguaje que intento hacer significativo para ti, la forma en que toda la experiencia humana se enriquece si simplemente seguimos los Diez Mandamientos? (Esta disciplina se puede encontrar de una forma u otra en las escrituras de toda religión, lo que sugiere la igualdad entre todas las razas y religiones).

Buenas noches y buena suerte
Gracias, JR (John Ratkovich)
JR@TheFutureBelongsToMe.com

www.TheFutureBelongsToMe.com

Notes